Antique Trader®

Black Americana

Price Guide

D1216632

Kyle Husfloen, editor

Leonard Davis, contributing editor

Caroline Torem-Craig, photographer

©2005 KP Books
Published by

kp books

An imprint of F+W Publications, Inc.

700 East State Street • Iola, WI 54990-0001
715-445-2214 • 888-457-2873

Our toll-free number to place an order or obtain
a free catalog is (800) 258-0929.

On the cover: Gilner Mammy busts, each 11 inches high,
unmarked, valued at $1,200-$1,300 each.

Library of Congress Catalog Number: 2004093902

ISBN: 0-87349-819-4

Designed by Kay Sanders
Edited by Kyle Husfloen

Printed in United States of America

Table of Contents

ACKNOWLEDGMENTS

It has been nearly 10 years since the first edition of the *Antique Trader Black Americana Price Guide* appeared in bookstores, and I'm very pleased to be able to present here the completely updated and expanded edition to that popular work.

The marketplace for Black Americana has continued to grow and expand in recent years, and this new edition offers an even better overview of this field with a wider range of antiques and collectibles included. In addition, it is especially exciting to present this updated edition in ALL COLOR. Although our first edition did include a selection of color photos, this edition offers readers the unique op-portunity to see hundreds more pieces in full color. They say a picture is worth a thousand words, so pictures in color must be worth several thousand.

What has made this project even more enjoyable for me is the fact that my two major collaborators on the first volume have again been intimately in-volved in this project. Collector and ex-pert Leonard Davis has provided hundreds of new listings and graciously allowed our associate, Caroline Torem-Craig, to use her professional photogra-phy skills to capture beautiful color imag-es of prized pieces in his collection. This volume wouldn't have been possible without their invaluable input and the ex-

Caroline Torem-Craig (seen at far left with Lil Kim at a tribute to the Notorious B.I.G.) is the party photo editor at Paper and PM magazines and writes a column called "Cultural Sushi – 'N.Y. Nightlife Served Hot.'" She is about to launch a new magazine with Jake Torem called Fashionland, soon to be accessed at www.fashionland.org, and she and Leonard Davis are about to produce a charitable project called "99 Josephine Bakers." Reach her by e-mail at nynightclub-bing@yahoo.com.

pert skills of my contributing editors, and I offer them my sincerest heartfelt thanks.

Although the Leonard Davis Collection provides the core of our listings here, I also must note the gracious help of several other dealers and collectors who also allowed us to use photographs and descriptions of pieces from their collections. Among these individuals were Roger Chin, Brenda Schane, Eve Savitt, Laura Craig, Ken Leach Gallery 47, Mr. A. Karim of John Walker Antiques and Objets de Vertu, Jack Peapopa of Rare Records and Charles Reynolds of Reynolds Toys.

For other photographs and information on black collectibles, we must also acknowledge the following collectors, dealers and auction houses:

Charlton Hall Galleries, Columbia, S.C.; Christie's, New York, N.Y.; Collectors Auction Services, Oil City, Pa.; Kerra Davis, Blackshear, Ga.; Susan Eberman, Bedford, Ind.; Garth's Auctions, Inc., Delaware, Ohio; Green Valley Auctions, Mt. Crawford, Va.; Jackson's Auctions, Cedar Falls, Iowa; James D. Julia, Fairfield, Maine; Gary Kirsner Auctions, Coral Springs, Fla.; McMasters-Harris Premier Doll Auctions, Cambridge, Ohio; Neal Auction Co., New Orleans, La.; New Orleans Auction Galleries, New Orleans, La.; Richard Opfer Auctioneering, Inc., Timonium, Md.; Parker-Braden Auctions, Carlsbad, N.M.; Past Tyme Pleasures, Los Altos, Calif.; David Rago Auctions, Lambertville, N.J.; Slater's Americana, Inc., Indianapolis, Ind.; Swann Galleries, New York, N.Y.; Temples Antiques, Eden Prairie, Minn.; Tradewinds Antiques, Manchester-by-the-Sea, Mass.

It has been a real pleasure to work on this brand new and greatly expanded edition of a price guide that covers one of the most fascinating fields of collecting today. I hope all those who were kind enough to lend their time and talents will be proud of the results. This is a book that is sure to prove an invaluable reference and guide for years to come. Thank you all and enjoy.

Kyle Husfloen, Editor

Collecting Black Americana

Leonard Davis, contributing editor of Antique Trader's Black Americana Price Guide

My name is Leonard Davis and I am a proud collector of Black Americana. I would like to thank Antique Trader Books for providing me with this opportunity to share my knowledge and experience as an advanced collector and allowing me to showcase my pride, passion and magnificent obsession. As you observe the objects and images in this book and evaluate their significance and monetary value, you may also realize that these relics are a testimony of the way things once were, the gradual changes that have been made, and the hope of changes to come.

My journey as a collector began about 20 years ago while watching a cable TV program that featured a cleaning service. In the program several cleaning women shared their experiences with the homes they cleaned. They pointed out that although they seldom met the occupants of the homes they worked in,

they could usually determine the ethnic heritage of the homeowner by observing the artifacts and adornments decorating the homes. However, there was one striking exception to this rule: African Americans. The cleaning women noted that, typically, black people do not decorate their homes with images that reflect their heritage and culture.

I immediately looked throughout my home and realized that I was also guilty. *There were no black images in my home!* I was so ashamed that I immediately removed all the fish, flowers and abstract art from my walls and tables, determined to replace them with black imagery.

A friend suggested that I begin my search for black images at the local flea market, a haven for rare and unusual finds. On the following Saturday I went to the flea market. I approached a few dealers and explained that I was searching for black images to embellish my home and didn't know where to begin. After sorting through tons of antiques that

Kellogg's Corn Flakes box featuring image of Willie Mays

Josephine Banker serving tray

day, I bought a McCoy mammy cookie jar for $25, three sets of salt and pepper shakers for $10 each, and a book, *The Uncalled*, by Paul Lawrence Dunbar, the famous poet, for $30. I couldn't wait to get home and put my new treasures on display. I was so excited that I called my family and friends and asked them all to please start combing the flea markets and antique stores for black artifacts; I wanted to fill up my whole apartment with black images. I had set out on a mission to find a few black images and

artifacts to decorate my home, but what I found opened a whole new chapter in my life: I became a collector!

Like other enthusiasts, collectors are driven by their passion for a particular object, image or topic; exposure to the full range of items to enable them to know what to look for; a burning desire to seek and find the rarest of the rare; and knowledge, which enables them to purchase wisely. I already had the passion and the desire; all I needed was the knowledge and the exposure.

After several trips to the flea market, I began to seek other sources for finding Black Americana. The *Antique Trader* newspaper was a particularly helpful resource for finding books on collectibles and access to dealers, antique malls and auctions. Advice from experienced collectors and dealers also proved to be invaluable.

The first collector/dealer I met was Melinda Saunders. She and her partner, Jeannette Carson, produced Black Collectible shows in Silver Springs, Md.,

Figural tobacco jar

Cast-iron mammy wall clock

Segregation era "Colored Seats Balconey (sic)" sign

during the 1980s and invited me to come. When I attended my first black Americana show, I went "hog wild" and bought everything in sight: dolls, toys, quilts, ephemera, clocks, games, sports, fine art, folk art and kitchen items. I came home with a carload of collectibles. After I spent my rent money, food money, and gas money, I used credit cards, postdated checks, and then IOUs. Well ... that's what obsession can do to you.

Black images can be found in practically every collecting category — dolls, toys, quilts, ephemera, clocks, games, sports, fine art, folk art, kitchen items — the list is endless. After being exposed to such a broad range of collectible items, I found that I had a particular attraction to cookie jars, kitchen items, and tobacco

humidors. I loved the fact that these artifacts, which appear as sculptures, are also utilitarian items. This led to creating a wish list of rare items that I was determined to find; even though searching for rare artifacts can become a lifelong quest, I was committed.

One very important aspect of collecting involves knowing the difference between an original and a reproduction. It is imperative that you learn how to determine the age and authenticity of items *before you buy them*! Look for details such as the artist's signature, labels, logos, correct dimensions, and colors. Don't be afraid to ask the dealer for proof of age and authenticity. It's also important to have reference books, price guides and friends who are knowledgeable collectors to refer to when in doubt.

I remember an incident in which I was about to purchase a very rare and expensive advertisement. The dealer claimed that the ad was original and dated back to the 1920s. But, I noticed a zip code at the bottom of the poster. Luckily, I remembered that zip codes weren't implemented until 1963, which meant the dealer was either misinformed or being dishonest. In either case, my knowledge saved me from buying what turned out to be a reproduction.

Gold Dust Washing powder containers

Another important factor to consider is condition, condition, condition! Even if the object is rare and original, the value of an object is determined by its condition. Carefully inspect items before you buy them: look for chips, cracks, dings, tears, spots, repairs, missing pages, bottoms without tops, mismatched sets. Let the buyer beware; arm yourself with knowledge!

I expanded my frame of reference by attending antique shows, swap meets, antique auctions, and the Internet (eBay). My occupation as a fashion designer fortunately allows me to travel to different countries. I frequently shop the flea markets of Paris, which is where I found my Josephine Baker posters and photos. I also frequent the famous Portobello Road flea market in London, which is a great place to find rare banks, dolls and humidors. My search has also extended into Canada, Australia, South America and the Virgin Islands. I corresponded with antiques dealers and exchanged photos, information and resources.

As I attended more shows and met other collectors, I realized that some collectors are very focused and only collect in certain specified categories. Relics from the Civil Rights movement, slavery, and other black historical items are often the centerpiece for Black Americana collections. Can you imagine the elation of owning a letter written by Harriet Tubman, a pressing comb belonging to Madame C.J. Walker, or Martin Luther

A variety of Aunt Jemima products atop a rare Aunt Jemima griddle

"Jolly Nigger with Top Hat" mechanical bank

If you collect cookie jars, ceramic figurines, and salt and pepper shakers, you will notice that many of these items bear the marking "made in Japan," "Occupied Japan" or simply "Japan." Shortly after Japan's defeat in World War II in 1945, America proposed a free trade agreement to help Japan rebuild its industries. Since clay (for the pottery industry) was that country's most accessible material, Japan flooded the American market with knickknacks and ceramic objects. Many of these utilitarian kitchen items were made in the image of black people. I was curious as to why so many of them have such distorted features, i.e. bulging eyes, big red lips, big flat noises, and ethnic anomalies like jet black skin with blond hair, big lips and blue eyes. Interestingly, the Japanese artist created these exaggerated images based on verbal descriptions and cartoon caricatures, which were considered at that time to be cute and humorous depictions of people of African decent.

King's autograph? Other major categories include music (records and CDs), black theater, movie posters, sports, and black militaria. And don't forget rare books, autographs, coins, postage stamps and original paintings. I was greatly honored to meet Dr. Sample Pittman, who has the world's largest collection of Civil Rights items and slave shackles; and Elizabeth Meaders, the famous collector of black sports and military collectibles. Other individuals who have made an impression on me include Rose Fontanella, my mentor and friend; Gloria Lowery Tyrrell, who dons period costumes and performs impersonations of historical black icons; and Roger Lewis, who collects and produces Black Americana cookie jars. I cannot forget collector and author Jan Lindenberger, who encouraged me to do this book.

As my own collection grew, I began to ponder who was responsible for creating some of these stereotypical — and sometimes derogatory — images, and whether these images really reflect the true lives and history of black people. What impressions did these artisans intended to convey?

Author Leonard Davis holds a string holder promoting Coon-Chicken Inn

Brayton-Laguana "Maid" cookie jar

There are a variety of ways that one may interpret these artifacts, as the civil rights leader Julian Bond so eloquently noted in the first volume of this book (*Black Americana Price Guide,* Antique Trader Books, 1996):

We collectors have many motives for our obsession. ... For some, they embrace a fascination with an American yesterday, a before-civil rights era when it was thought proper to decorate homes with cute and cruel depictions of the "other" — the grinning caricatures and twisted bodies of our fellow Americans of African descent. ... For others, like myself, these artifacts also summon up yesterday's world, but in our hands and homes they become reminders of a different sort. They speak of triumph and overcoming, and inform us that despite what others thought and believed, we were never what these figurines and objects suggest. We see them as sentinels guarding the past, doorkeepers who prevent our ever returning to it, harsh — if even sometimes beautiful — preservers of the history we have overthrown.

Some collectors and dealers label these items as Black Memorabilia. I take offense at that reference because these items reflect the distorted attitude America once held toward people of African decent. To simply call these items "memorabilia" trivializes the negative impact that these stereotypical images have had on an entire race of people who have endured years of humiliation and second class treatment. Both the negative and positive images are truly a part of the rich history that makes up America and rightfully should be referred to as "Americana," not "memorabilia." However, collectors still find it difficult to view some of these items as having historical significance; they see them only as negative depictions of black people and think they should be destroyed or hidden from view.

I feel that these artifacts are tangible evidence of a period in history when African Americans were not in control of their own imagery. Black collectible artifacts document the evolution of the African American image as told through black dolls, banks, toys, cookie jars and postcards, some of them dating as far back as the mid-1800s. They also document the emergence of advocacy organizations like the NAACP, which demanded that "People of Color" no longer tolerate derogatory cultural references such as "nigger," "coon" and "Sambo" or inferior images such as fat, do-rag-wearing mammies and watermelon-eating, red-lipped, bug-eyed spooks.

As your collection grows and matures and you near completion of your collector's wish list, you may then become what is considered a "collector/custodian." A great debt is owed to the collector/custodians because most of these cherished artifacts that we collect would never have survived through the years if it were not for the custodians who have properly maintained and preserved them. I was excited to learn that a great number of celebrities have a passion for collecting Black Americana: Whoopi Goldberg, who collects kitchen items, figurines and historical documents; Oprah Winfrey, who collects dolls, paintings, quilts and books; Bill Cosby, who collects paintings and sculptures; and Julian Bond, who collects books, Civil Rights era documents and photos.

Several books on the subject of collecting Black Americana have been published to date, but most of them express the historian's point of view. It is not my intention to portray myself as a historian; I am simply one of the many crazed and obsessed Black Americana collectors and this is my magnificent obsession. I hope that this book will encourage you to start collecting while inspiring you to appreciate the importance of preserving African American history.

— Leonard Davis

Leonard's Top 10 Favorites

- Aunt Jemima cooking griddle
- Josephine Baker serving tray
- Segregation signs
- Figural tobacco jars
- Coon-Chicken Inn string holder
- Brayton-Laguana "Maid" cookie jar
- Cast-iron Mammy wall clock
- "Jolly Nigger High Hat" mechanical bank
- Gold Dust Washing Powder containers
- Willie Mays Kellogg's Corn Flakes box

Leonard Davis currently resides in New York City. He is a writer, event planner, producer, artist, and fashion designer. A graduate of the Fashion Institute of Technology, and also a graduate of the famous "Ecole De La Chambre Syndicale Couture" Paris, France, Leonard has worked for Willi Smith, Liz Claiborne, Josephine Chaus, Ashley Stewart, "Home Shopping Network" and QVC. Leonard has written many articles on collecting Black Americana, has appeared in magazine and newspaper articles, and has been featured on numerous TV programs showcasing his Black Americana collection, including Fox Network's "Personal FX," "The Antiques Road Show," "Treasures In Your Home," "Antique Show and Sell," and HDTV's "Magnificent Obsessions." Leonard continues to travel the world and search for new items to add to his collection.

— Chapter 1 —

ADVERTISING ITEMS

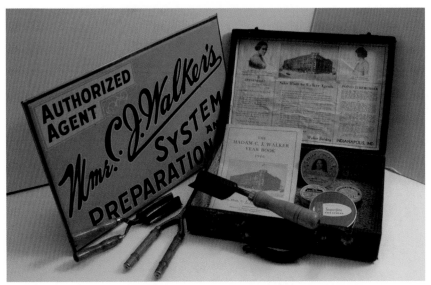

Mme. C.J. Walker Complete Agent's Kit

Beauty agent kit, "Mme. C.J. Walker's System," authorized agent's kit for Madame Walker's School of Beauty Culture, which agents received free upon graduation, contains hair care preparation, pressing comb, agent sign & promotional materials, ca. 1920s, the complete set (ILLUS. above) **$2,600**

Beauty agent kit box only, "The Mme. C.J. Walker's Mfg. Co., Inc," ca. 1920's, (illus. above) **$2,600,**

Beauty agent kit inside cover label,, "The Mme. C.J. Walker Mfg. Co.,

Interior Label from Walker Agent Kit Box

Inc.," information on its beauty
school w/view of its headquarters &
two ladies, includes details on official certificate of graduation each
student would receive, ca. 1920s
(ILLUS. bottom previous page) **300**

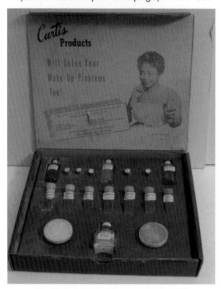

Curtis Products Demonstration Kit

Beauty products demonstration kit,
"Curtis Products," fitted box includes
various facial products in sample sizes, A.W. Curtis Laboratories, Detroit,
Michigan, ca. 1940s (ILLUS.) **225**

Early "Cottolene" Recipe Booklet

Booklet, "Cottolene," color cover
scene of a smiling black girl standing & holding armful of fresh cotton,
contains various recipes using Cottolene Shortening, early 1900s
(ILLUS.) **30-50**

Booklet, die-cut, "Aunt Jemima's Special Cake & Pastry Flour," recipe-
type, in the shape of the product
box, 1906, 3 1/4 x 4 7/8" (ILLUS.
below) **175-200**

Early Aunt Jemima Recipe Booklet

*Cover from the Fairbank's Gold Dust
Twins Booklet*

*Page from the Fairbank's Gold Dust
Twins Booklet*

*Page from the Fairbank's Gold Dust
Twins Booklet*

Booklet, "Fairbank's Drawing and
Painting Book Showing The Gold
Dust Twins at Work and Play," all-
color, sketched by E.W. Kemble,
copyrighted in 1904, cover & two inner pages shown, the complete
booklet (ILLUS. of cover & illustra-
tions) **75-100**

Booklet, "Lactated Food for Infants
and Invalids," cover features a little
black boy sitting on a package of
lactated foods, titled "Afrie's Sable
Scion" .... **50+**

Aunt Jemima Recipe Booklet

Booklet, "Tempting New Aunt Jemima Pancake 'n Waffle Recipes!,"
color cover picture of Aunt Jemima,
1950s (ILLUS.) **40-50**

Early Green River Whiskey Bottle & Box

Bottle, "Green River Whiskey," clear glass w/paper labels, produced in Canada, 1935, w/original box, 1 qt., 8 1/2" h. (ILLUS. above) **250**

Bottle, "Green River Whiskey," display-type, clear glass w/paper label, 1935, 2 1/2 gal. size, 20" h. (ILLUS. of front & back below) **400**

Front and Back Views of Rare Large Green River Whiskey Bottle

Rare "Bamboo Coons" Candy Box

Candy box, cardboard, "Bamboo Coons - National Candy Co. Detroit," rectangular, the lid in black & white w/border of bamboo sticks framing scene of a chubby African native child perched on a vine, the sides of the box decorated w/heads of other children, late 19th - early 20th c., unlisted, rare, light overall soiling, 6 1/2 x 9", 2 1/4" h. (ILLUS. of two views, above)........................... **754**

Candy box, cardboard, "Heide's Colored Coons," five-pound box, long dance scene on the cover, dated June 1906 (ILLUS. below)................. **400**

"Heide's Colored Coons" Candy Box

Views of a Whitman's Pickaninny Peppermints Box

Candy box, cov., cardboard, "Whitman's Pickaninny Peppermints - Chocolate Covered," shows black children's heads on a narrow, long box, early 20th c., 2 3/8 oz.. (ILLUS. of two views, above) **450**

Candy box, cov., the cover w/label featuring scene of black boy & girl on teeter-totter made from peppermint stick, excellent condition, large ... **400**

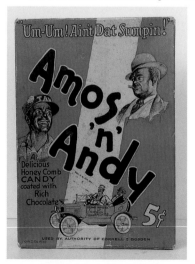

Amos 'n' Andy Candy Box

Candy box w/original cover, cardboard, "Amos 'n' Andy," w/heads of the characters & the Freshair Taxi shown, orange & white w/black lettering, ca. 1930 (ILLUS.) **250-300**

Early Cream of Wheat Cereal Box

Cereal box, cardboard, "Cream of Wheat," picture of the chef w/a long ladle & bowl of cereal, ca. 1920, soiled, damaged (ILLUS.).................. **250**

"Choco Maizoro" Mexican Cereal Box

Cereal box, "Choco Maizoro," caricature cartoon images of black children on the front, Mexico, 1979 (ILLUS. left) **100**

Cereal box, "Cream of Wheat Enriched 5 Minute," cardboard, 1 lb. 12 oz. size, ca. 1940s (ILLUS. second from left with other containers, bottom of page).................................... **95**

Cereal box, "Cream of Wheat - Enriched 5 Minute," cardboard, 14 oz. size, ca. 1940s (ILLUS. far left with other containers, below) **55**

Cereal box, "Cream of Wheat - Quick," cardboard, 14 oz. size, ca. 1960s (ILLUS. second from right with other containers, below)............... **60**

Cereal box, "Cream of Wheat - Quick," cardboard, small sample size of 14 oz. size, ca. 1960s (ILLUS. top right with four other containers, below)............................ **100**

Five Various Packages of Cream of Wheat

Cereal Box with Derek Jeter Photo

Cereal box, "Jeter's Frosted Flakes,"
cover picture of Derek Jeter, 1999,
20 oz. size, near mint (ILLUS.) **35**

Roberto Clemente Corn Flakes Box

Cereal box, "Kellogg's Corn Flakes,"
cover photo of Roberto Clemente,
1992, 18 oz. size, near mint (ILLUS.)..... **45**

Corn Flakes Box with Young Black Boy

Cereal box, "Kellogg's Corn Flakes,"
cover photo of a young black boy
eating the cereal, from the "Every-
day People" series, 1980, 1 lb., 2
oz. size, near mint (ILLUS.) **35**

Houston Comets Corn Flakes Box

Cereal box, "Kellogg's Corn Flakes,"
cover photo of the Houston Comets
team commemorating the inaugural
WNBA Championship, 1997, 12 oz.
size, near mint (ILLUS.)........................ **75**

Olympic Dream Team on Cereal Box

Cereal box, "Kellogg's Corn Flakes," cover photo of the U.S. Olympic Gold Medal basketball "Dream Team," 1992, near mint (ILLUS.) **75**

Vanessa Williams Corn Flakes Box

Cereal box, "Kellogg's Corn Flakes," front photo of Vanessa Williams as Miss America, 1984, near mint (ILLUS.) **200**

Another Dream Team Cereal Box

Cereal box, "Kellogg's Corn Flakes," cover photo of the U.S. Olympic Gold Medal basketball "Dream Team" standing w/hands on hearts, 1992, near mint (ILLUS.) **75**

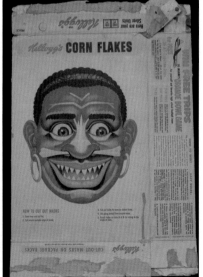

Corn Flakes Box with African Mask

Cereal box, "Kellogg's Corn Flakes," mask of African savage on the back, 1953, 1 lb. 2 oz. size, near mint (ILLUS.) **100**

Corn Flakes Box with Mammy Mask

Corn Flakes Box with Willie Mays Offer

Cereal box, "Kellogg's Corn Flakes," smiling black Mammy cut-out mask on the back, one of ten masks you could collect, 1940, 8 oz. size, near mint (ILLUS.)...................................... **100**

Cereal box, "Kellogg's Corn Flakes," special offer for Willie Mays base-ball cards, 1972, 8 oz. size, near mint (ILLUS. of the box back)............. **300**

Cereal box, "Kellogg's Corn Pops," special offer for four Jackson 5 stickers inside, 1984, near mint (ILLUS. below and top of next page) **200**

Back of Corn Pops Cereal Box with Jackson 5 Sticker Offer

*Front of Corn Pops Cereal Box with
Jackson 5 Sticker Offer*

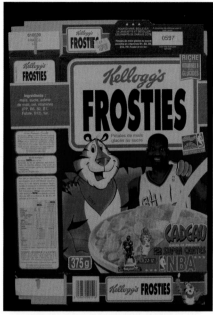

French Frosties Box with Olajuwon

Cereal box, "Kellogg's Frosties," French version of Frosted Flakes w/cover photo of Hakeem Olajuwon, 1996, 20 oz. size, near mint (ILLUS.) **40**

Maurice Green & Marion Jones on Box

Cereal box, "Kellogg's Frosted Flakes," cover photos of track & field Olympic stars Maurice Green & Marion Jones noted as the fastest man & woman in the world, 2000, 1 lb. 2 oz. size, near mint (ILLUS.) **45**

Early Korn-Kinks Corn Flakes Box

Cereal box, "Korn-Kinks Malted Corn Flakes," cardboard, features large sketch of Kornelia Kinks on the front, The H-O Company, Buffalo, New York, ca. 1900 (ILLUS. previous page) **900**

Cereal box, "Post Frosted Rice Krispies," Jackson 5 free cut-out record on the back, 9 oz. size, near mint (ILLUS. bottom previous column) ... **300**

Quaker Mr. T Cereal Box

Cereal box, "Quaker Mr. T. Cereal," large image of Mr. T. on front, 1984, 9 1/2 oz. size, near mint (ILLUS.) **75**

Tiger Woods on French Wheaties Box

Cereal box, "Maple Frosted Wheaties," French version, cover picture of Tiger Woods, 1997, 18 oz. size, near mint (ILLUS.) **45**

Jackson 5 on Frosted Rice Krispies Box

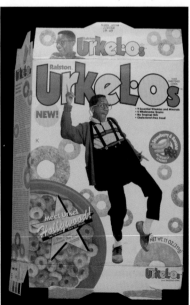

Ralston-Purina Urkel.Os Cereal Box

Cereal box, "Ralston-Purina Ur-kel.Os" cereal, photo of the TV char-acter from "Family Matters" on the front, 1991, 11 oz. size, near mint (ILLUS. previous page) **55**

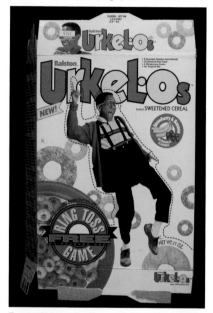

Front of Urkel.Os Box with Ring Toss Game

Back of Urkel.Os Box with Ring Toss Game

Cereal box, "Ralston-Purina Ur-kel.Os" cereal, "Ring Toss Games" offer, photo of the TV character from

"Family Matters" on the front & back, 1988, 11 oz. size, near mint (ILLUS. of front & back) **55**

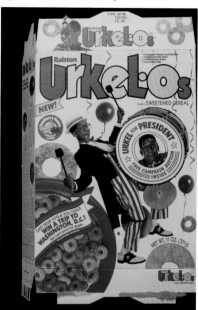

1992 Urkel.Os Cereal Box

Cereal box, "Ralston-Purina Ur-kel.Os" cereal, "Urkel for President," photo of the TV character from "Family Matters" on the front, 1992, 11 oz. size, near mint (ILLUS.) **55**

Sammy Sosa on Cereal Box

Cereal box, "Slammin' Sammy's Frosted Flakes," cover picture of Sammy Sosa, 1999, 20 oz. size, near mint (ILLUS. previous page) **35**

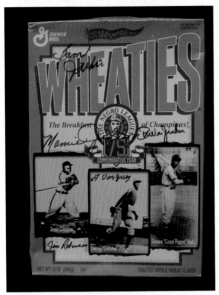

Wheaties Special Negro League Box

Cereal box, "Wheaties," commemorating Negro League Baseball's 75th Anniversary, cover photos of early players, 1989, 12 oz. size (ILLUS.)

Front of Michael Jordan Wheaties Box

Back of Michael Jordan Wheaties Box

Cereal box, "Wheaties," cover & back photos of Michael Jordan, 1989, 18 oz. size, near mint (ILLUS. of front & back) **55**

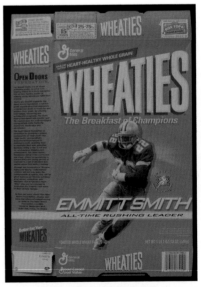

Emmitt Smith Wheaties Box

Cereal box, "Wheaties," cover photo of Emmitt Smith, 2002, 1 lb. 2 oz. size, near mint (ILLUS.) **45**

Michael Jordan Jump Shot Box

Cereal box, "Wheaties," cover picture of Michael Jordan in leaping jump shot pose, second in a series, 1988, 18 oz. size, near mint (ILLUS.) **100**

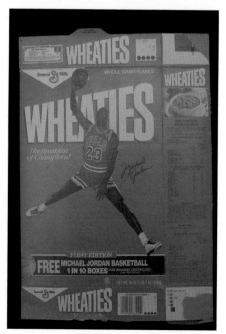

Michael Jordan Spread Eagle Box

Cereal box, "Wheaties," cover picture of Michael Jordan in leaping spread-eagle pose, first in a series, 1987, 18 oz. size, near mint (ILLUS.) **150**

Jordan on Single Serving Wheaties Box

Cereal box, "Wheaties," cover picture of Michael Jordan, single-serving size, near mint (ILLUS.) **40**

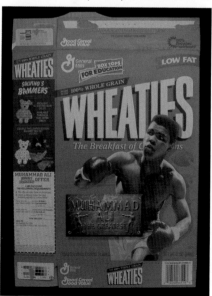

Wheaties Box with Muhammad Ali

Cereal box, "Wheaties," cover picture
of Muhammad Ali, subtitled "The
Greatest," 1999, near mint (ILLUS.
previous page) **55**

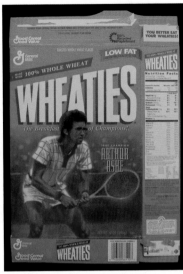

Arthur Ashe on Wheaties Box

Cereal box, "Wheaties," cover picture
of tennis star Arthur Ashe, subtitled
"True Champion," 1995, 12 oz. size,
near mint (ILLUS.) **55**

Althea Gibson on Wheaties Box

Cereal box, "Wheaties," cover picture
of Olympic star Althea Gibson, subtitled "A True Pioneer," 2001, 12 oz.
size, near mint (ILLUS.) **55**

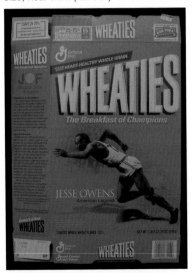

Wheaties Jesse Owens Cereal Box

Cereal box, "Wheaties," cover picture
of Olympic star Jesse Owens, subtitled "American Legend," 2003, 1 lb.,
2 oz. size, near mint (ILLUS.) **55**

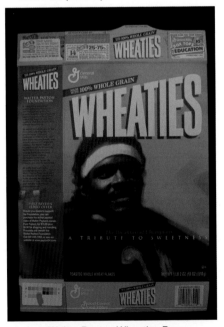

Walter Payton Wheaties Box

Cereal box, "Wheaties," cover picture
of Walter Payton, subtitled "Tribute
to Sweetness," 1999, 1 lb. 2 oz.
size, near mint (ILLUS.) **45**

Large Group of Cream of Wheat Boxes

Cereal boxes, "Cream of Wheat," cardboard, various sizes & ages, early to mid-20th c. (ILLUS. of group) **60-300**

Cereal container, "Cream of Wheat - Quick," tin can, cylindrical, 1 lb. 2 oz. size, ca. 1960s (ILLUS. far right, bottom, with other containers, bottom page 19)...................................... **100**

Cleanser box, cardboard, "Fairbank's Gold Dust Washing Powder," pictures the Twins, black & orange, ca. 1920s, 4 x 6" (ILLUS.) **250**

"Fun-to-Wash Washing Powder" Box

Cleanser box, cardboard, "Fun-to-Wash Washing Powder," picture of Mammy's head, sample-size, Hygienic Laboratories, Buffalo, N.Y. (ILLUS.) **100**

Fairbank's Gold Dust Box

Doll, die-cut cardboard figure of black Mammy w/yellow & red kerchief on her head & wearing a white apron over a red dress, yellow & silver oval sticker at waist reads "Net Weight 1 lb.," giveaway from a candy company, early 20th c. .... **25+**

Madam Walker Face Powder Container

Face powder container, round, paper, "Madam C.J. Walker Superfine Face Powder," ca. 1950s (ILLUS.) ... **100**

Famous Amos Cookie Bags

Famous Amos cookie bag, paper, large 16 oz. size, label w/photo of Wally Amos (ILLUS. left with small bag) **15**

Famous Amos cookie bag, paper, small 2 1/4 oz. size, label w/photo of Wally Amos (ILLUS. right with large cookie bag) **25**

Famous Amos Glass Display Jar

Famous Amos Cookies display jar, round, clear glass w/printed logo, large star w/"Super Star," 1990s (ILLUS.) **125**

Rare St. Louis World's Fair Fan

Fan, round cardboard hand-type, color scene of the St. Louis World's Fair, 1904, featuring the Gold Dust Twins at the bottom edge, flat wooden handle (ILLUS.) **500**

Sample Size Aunt Jemima Flour Box

Rare "Bakerfix Brilliantine" Box

Flour box, cardboard, sample-size, "Aunt Jemima Buckwheat, Corn & Wheat Flour," ca. 1917, 4 oz. (ILLUS.) **300**

Hair cream box, cardboard, "Bakerfix Brilliantine," red, white & black w/sketch of Josephine Baker & handsome man, France, ca. 1920s-30s (ILLUS. top next column)... **500**

Hair pressing comb, turned wood handle, steel comb, Madam C.J. Walker name marked on the comb, early 20th c. (ILLUS. below & part of kit page 13).. **350**

Ink blotter, advertising "Besse, Mills & Co. - Clothiers and Furnishers," rectangular card w/color scene of crying black baby suspended by shirt from flowering branch, wording around the yellow border band, ca. 1900, England (ILLUS. next page) **25**

Madam C.J. Walker Hair Pressing Comb

Early Aunt Jemima Die-cut Mask

Early Advertising Ink Blotter

Mask, die-cut cardboard, Halloween-type, face of Aunt Jemima wearing a red bandanna w/white wording, further advertising on the back, 1902-16 (ILLUS. top next column) **350-400**

Matchbook, "Sambo's Restaurant," Little Black Sambo & Tiger pictured...... **25**

Menu, "Dinah's Restaurant," real photo reproduced on the cover, Palo Alto, California .... **50+**

Photograph of beauty school & supply store, black & white exterior view of the Mme. C.J. Walker School of Beauty Culture & the beauty supply store, the staff members posed in front, St. Louis, Missouri, ca. 1920s (ILLUS. below).... **200**

Exterior Photo of Walker School of Culture School & Supply Store

Early Gold Dust Pinback Button

Pinback button, celluloid, "Gold Dust Washing Powder," color design of large crossed American flags against white background above black & gold logo w/Gold Dust twins, red & blue wording reads "The Best Flag - The Best Cleaner. - You Can't Beat Them!," ca. 1898, 1 1/4" d. (ILLUS.) **193**

Pinback button, souvenir from Manny's Shanty, Atlanta, Georgia **15-20**

Postcard, Korn Kinks Cereal, from the series titled "Jocular Jinks of Kornelia Kinks," H-O Company, Buffalo, New York, color, shows Kornelia on stilts w/box of cereal under her arm, another girl pulling a kite string & about to pull over Kornelia, caption reads "You Smash Dem Kinks I'll Spoil You' Face Chile," a cabin in the background, two versions available, each .... **25+**

Postcards, "Gold Dust Washing Powder," set of four, each w/a color scene of the Gold Dust Twins in various poses, early 20th c., the set (ILLUS. below) **75**

Print, titled "The Jackson Wagon Sun Flower Band - As they appeared at the Great Fairs of 1884," color lithographed outdoor scene of the all-male black band in a group in front of a Jackson wagon, inset photo of band leader in upper left, in early veneered frame, print 8 1/4 x 10 1/2" (small edge tear, minor veneer chips on frame) **231**

Puppet toy, "Atwater Kent Radio - 'Jolly Dancing Figure,'" uncut light cardboard figure of a black minstrel in a striped colorful outfit, reverse w/little radio ads (very slight foxing) **75**

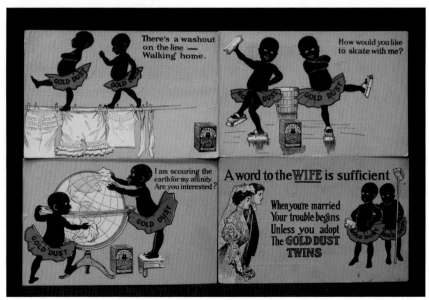

Set of Four Gold Dust Twins Postcards

Two Early Aunt Jemima String Puzzles

Puzzle, skill-type, pinback round metal disk-form w/clear top, caricature of a black woman's head inside shown wearing a red dress, pearl necklace & red earrings against a yellow background, small white beads to roll into indentations, reads around the edges "Use Star Soap - Schultz & Co. Zanesville, O.," excellent condition w/some rim damage, early 20th c. .... **50+**

Puzzle, string-type, die-cut cardboard, smiling bust of Aunt Jemima, marked "Use Aunt Jemima Flour," ca. 1905-16 (ILLUS. above left with other puzzle) **150**

Puzzle, string-type, die-cut cardboard, smiling bust of Aunt Jemima, marked "Use Aunt Jemima Flour," ca. 1905-16 (ILLUS. above right with other puzzle) **200**

Rice box, "Uncle Ben's Original Converted Rice" cover photo of Hakeem Olajuwon, 2 lb. size, 1997 (ILLUS. right) **95**

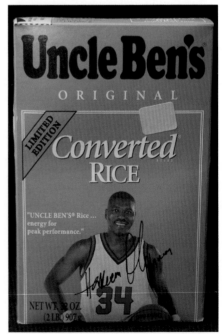

Olajuwon on Uncle Ben's Rice Box

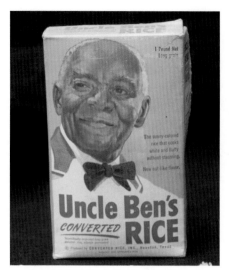

Original Uncle Ben's Rice Box

Rice box, "Uncle Ben's Original Converted Rice" traditional box illustration of smiling Uncle Ben, 1 lb. size, 1950s (ILLUS.)..................................... **125**

Scouring powder can, "Fairbanks Gold Dust Scouring Powder," cardboard, 15 oz. size (ILLUS. second from right with other Gold Dust containers, below) **125**

Scouring powder can, "Fairbanks Gold Dust Scouring Powder," cardboard, sample size (ILLUS. below second from left with three other Gold Dust containers) **200**

Sign, "Aunt Jemima Pancake Flour," string-hung die-cut color-lithographed double-sided paper, large image of Aunt Jemima seated on swing w/plate of pancakes in her lap & packages of her flour beside her, early 20th c., foot creased, minor edge roughness, rare, 17 1/2" h. (ILLUS. below)................................ **4,747**

Rare Aunt Jemima Flour Hanger

Four Gold Dust Containers

Mme. C.J. Walker Agent Sign

Rare Automated Black Farmer Sign

Sign, "Authorized Agent - Mme. C.J. Walker's System and Preparations," printed tin, early 20th c. (ILLUS. above and part of kit page 13) **350**

Sign, automated, lithographed paper, half-length figure of black farmer wearing blue checkered shirt & worn overalls & brown rain hat, identical to version for Momenta but w/no advertising, winding the key causes the facial features to move, in original black wood frame, late 19th - early 20th c., small water stain on left ear, some flaking to white background, working, overall 21 x 26" (ILLUS. left) **3,450**

Primitive Painted Minstrel Show Sign

Sign, folk art painted wood type, "The Leroy Minstrels" in red across the pedimented top, painted w/primitive landscape scene centered by large figure of black man playing banjo, apparently on early Masonite w/stretcher structure in back, from New York State, early 20th c., repair to hand at top of banjo, hinge plate marks on the side, 35 x 40" (ILLUS. previous page) **3,450**

Trolley Card Sign with Gold Dust Twins

Sign, "Gold Dust," rectangular trolley card sign, color illustration of the Gold Dust twins wearing orange/red skirts reading "Gold Dust" in white, carrying box of soap & cleaning paraphernalia & walking toward a house w/a woman standing in front of it, trees & lawns in the background, "Gold Dust" in yellow at upper right, "For Spring House-cleaning" in light blue at lower left, rare, 14 1/2 x 25" (ILLUS.) **1,208**

Sign, "Paul Jones Distiller," color lithographed on rectangular wood, large scene entitled "The Temptations of St. Anthony," comical outdoor scene w/young black boy in the center & black woman holding huge slice of watermelon on the left & elderly black man holding bottle of whiskey on the right, cabin in background, ca. 1901, 13 3/4 x 20" (slight wear) **550**

"Picaninny Freeze" Ice Cream Sign

Sign, "Picaninny Freeze," rectangular cardboard printed in color w/a dark green background w/large yellow moon, grotesque caricature of a black child holding slice of watermelon, yellow, black, white & red wording reads "Eat Seeds 'n All! - Picaninny Freeze - 5¢ - A Pal For Your Palate," Henlers Ice Cream logo in corner, early 20th c., bright colors, unused condition, 11 x 14" (ILLUS.) **578**

Trade card, "'Bad Accident Bank," for an early mechanical bank, colorful scene showing black man seated in cart eating watermelon while a mule starts bucking to tip the cart, advertising on right side w/address of retailer in New York City, late 19th c. (toned edges, small closed right margin tear) **1,000**

Barretts' Dye House Trade Card

Trade card, "Barretts' Dye House," color scene of little white clown giving the boot to black shoeshine boy in minstrel outfit, reads "Send Your Feathers, Kid Gloves & Laces to Barretts' Dye House 52 Temple Place," England, late 1890s, 2 x 4" (ILLUS. previous page)..... **50+**

Trade card, "Base-Ball Bank - Patented," J. & E. Stevens Co., original card for "Darktown Battery" mechanical bank, brown & white, thin paper, ca. 1880s (tiny corner crease)................... **150**

New Household Range Card with Man

Trade card, "Buy New Household Ranges - White, Warner & Co., Taunton," large white rose blossom w/black man's head in center w/bee hovering above (ILLUS. left).............. **50+**

New Household Range Card with Boy

Trade card, "Buy New Household Ranges - White, Warner & Co., Taunton," large white rose blossom w/black boy's smiling head in center, late 19th c. (ILLUS.) .... **50+**

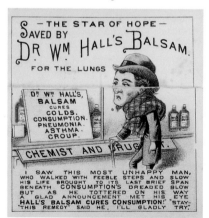

Trade card, "Dr. Wm. Hall's Balsam for the Lungs," folding-type, all-color, when closed shows sick white man in front of druggist's window, when open shows the healthy man w/his family & black Mammy in the background (ILLUS. closed & open, above & at right) .... **100+**

Two Views of the Hall's Balsam Card

Trade card, "Chase & Sanborn Coffee," folding-type, when closed reverse shows color scene of tiny Arab on horseback spoon feeding a huge comical black man's face from coffee cup, the front when closed shows stout white man, when opened inside shows winking black man holding can of coffee, includes list of coffees & characteristics, closed 3 x 4 3/4" (bit of pencil inside, outside soil, some bends) .... **50+**

Trade card, circus performer, "Millie-Christine - the Renowned - Two Headed Lady - 8th Wonder of the World," color drawing of famous late Victorian black Siamese twins, advertising on reverse .... **75+**

Trade card, "Clarence Brooks & Co. Varnishes New York," black comical subtitled "Darktown Fire Brigade - Hook and Ladder Practice," colorful (mild stain on right margin) **150**

Trade card, "Clarence Brooks & Co. Varnishes New York," black comical subtitled "Darktown Fire Brigade - Under Full Steam," colorful (tiny stain in one margin) **200**

Trade card, "Domestic Sewing Machine Company," scene of salesman calling on black woman in shanty, a goat eating his pants, ca. 1897 .... **50+**

Trade card, "Fairbanks Santa Claus Laundry Soaps," color lithograph showing Gold Dust Twins seated in a large wooden tub, ca. 1900, very rare (ILLUS. top right column) **200**

Trade card, "Fairbanks Soap," color lithograph showing Gold Dust Twins standing beside large wooden tub of steaming water, advertising on back, 3 1/2 x 5" .... **50+**

Trade card, "Fleishmann & Co's Compressed Yeast," card w/three vignettes, the left side w/boy carrying package of the product on his back, reads "See The Label - It Is Genuine," center scene of black Mammy cook, reads "It Is De Best," right side w/girl carrying

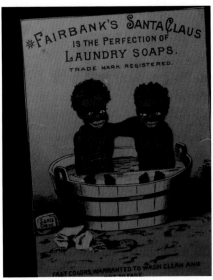

Rare Fairbanks Gold Dust Twins Card

package of baked goods, reads "Ask For Fleischmann & Co's Compressed Yeast," colorful, advertising on reverse (very light corner crease)......................... **80**

Trade card, "From Morgan's Confectionary," postcard-sized, black children on large peppermint stick seesaw **50**

Gold Dust Die-Cut Trade Card

French Feather Dyer Trade Card

Trade card, "Gold Dust Washing Powder," die-cut, classic color scene of Gold Dust Twins in wooden washtub (ILLUS. previous page) **150**

Trade card, "H. Methot - French Feather Dyer - 43 Winter St. Boston," all-color, shows black children riding around racetrack on ostriches, lead rider carrying red banner w/the advertising, a crowd & grandstand w/more advertising in background (ILLUS. above) **75**

Trade card, "Holbrook's Worcestershire Sauce," three-quarter length portrait of black Mammy carrying tray w/bottle of the product, reads across the bottom "Yes Honey, I'se Knows What's Good," finely printed & colorful w/advertising on reverse **200**

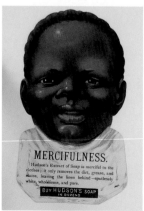

Hudson's Soap Trade Card

Trade card, "Hudson's Soap," shows large head of black baby above the word "Mercifulness" & other advertising (ILLUS.)...................................... **75**

Ivorine Soap Trade Card

Trade card, "Ivorine Soap," color scene of native woman scrubbing clothes by river while two children swim & an elephant holds a box of the product, reads across the bottom "Jes' What We's Been a Longin' For," J.B. Williams Co., 1900 (ILLUS.).. **75**

Trade Card with Snow Scene & Children

Trade card, "Jacob Bros. Pianos, Massachusetts," color front winter scene of three black children admiring snowman w/green wreath around its head (ILLUS.)...................... **50**

Trade card, "Kendall's Spavin Cure on Human Flesh," shows black jockey in horse race.............................. **40**

Trade card, "Lautz Brothers Soap," early color version w/scene of a mustached white man scrubbing face of black man turning white, wording on side of washtub reads "Beat That, If You Can - Lautz Bros' & Co's - Soaps - Buffalo, N.Y.," dated 1873... **150**

Trade card, "New York Dental Company," black cotton picker w/huge cotton bale on his head...................... **50+**

Trade card, real photo-type, smiling figure of black man wearing top hat & holding card reading "Compliments of J.r. Sullivan Furniture," printed on border "Ye Rose Studio - Conrad Building - Providence," late 19th c. (ILLUS. right)........................... **125**

Unusual Real Photo Trade Card

Trade card, "Rising Sun Stove Polish," color scene of angry black woman berating her husband for buying wrong stove blacking, reads "No Dinner?" above a long dialog across the bottom, 1890s (ILLUS. top next page) **10**

Rising Sun Stove Polish Comical Trade Card

Rising Sun Trade Card with Black Children

Trade card, "Rising Sun Stove Polish," color scene of group of black children w/ratty umbrella near cabin w/black couple outside, advertising on background gate reads "Rising Sun Stove Polish - Best in The World," caption along bottom in dialect reads "Hi Abe, Come under de breller! Does yer want to sunstruck yerself? De fremomiters gone up moren a foot," 1890s (ILLUS. above) **75**

Trade card, "Sanford's Ginger," shows black child holding carved watermelon w/another child in it **45**

Trade card, "Sapolio Soap," die-cut large head of cabbage w/face of a black child inside, Enoch Morgan & Sons (ILLUS. right) **40**

Sapolio Soap Card with Cabbage Child

Sapolio Soap Card with Watermelon

Trade card, "Sapolio Soap," large oval watermelon split open to reveal face of black child, Enoch Morgan & Sons (ILLUS. left) **40**

Trade card, "Stollwerck's Adler-Cacao," color outdoor winter scene of children in 17th century costume, one walking & carrying a package of chocolates, the other being pushed in sleigh by black servant while holding cylinder marked "Cacao," a dog walking alongside carrying carton of spilling candy, Germany, late 19th c., 2 x 4" (ILLUS. below)....... **45**

Trade card, "Stollwerck's Adler-Cacao," color scene of three white children pulling round box of candy w/black child wearing a crown & holding a branch of cacao beans sitting on it, Germany, late 19th c., 2 x 4" (ILLUS. bottom of page)............. **50**

Stollwerck's Card with Winter Scene

Stollwerck's Card with White Children Pulling a Box of Candy

Trade card, "Stump Speaker Bank," original trade card for the mechanical bank, advertising on the reverse w/a Chicago dealer's imprint, strong & bright colors, ca. 1880s (tiny speck near top of frame line) **1,400**

Trade card, "The Alden Fruit Vinegar," black comical of black man being knocked off ladder while picking apples as two dogs fight below, advertising on reverse **50**

Trade card, "The Alden Fruit Vinegar," black comical w/black girl sitting in old rocking chair holding baby & frightened by black man at the window eating watermelon, advertising on reverse.............. **50**

Universal Clothes Wringer Trade Card

Trade card, "The Universal Clothes Wringer," folding-type, sepia, black & white, scene w/black maid conversing w/her white mistress about the qualities of the new wringer, ca. 1870s (ILLUS.) **75**

Trade card, "Toe the Mark Shoes," colorful scene of black man carrying dead turkeys over his shoulders through the snow, reads across the top "Dey Say Dat Onesty am de Best Policy, but dis Yer Niggah Aint One of Dem as Allus Wants de Best," shoe advertising across the bottom, from a Gray's Lake, Illinois, store, 3 x 5 1/4" .... **50+**

Trade card, "W.E. Healy Boots and Shoes," two black shoeshine boys shine huge lady's shoe, reads "Go To W.E. Healy For Your Boots And Shoes - 181 Fourth St., Santa Rosa," colorful stock image....................... **35**

Trade card, "Wilson Reliable Yeast," comic scene of white woman & black cook watching as pan of dough rises out of covered pan above their heads, "The Wilson Reliable Yeast" across the top, a black dialect quote across the bottom .... **80+**

Trade cards, "Fairbank's Soaps," complete set of eight cards recounting "The History of the Fairbank's Twins," each card w/a different scene & advertising, the set (last card w/some stray red ink in margin)... **1,200**

One of a set of Tansill's Punch Cigar Trade Cards

Part of a set of Tansill's Punch Cigar Trade Cards

One of a set of Tansill's Punch Cigar Trade Cards

Trade cards, "Tansill's Punch - America's Finest 5¢ Cigar," a series featuring colored vignettes of idealized plantation life in the mid-19th century South, each scene w/tiny caption in the upper left corner including "A Cabin in The Good Old Time," "A Revival," "In the Land of Cotton," "Going to the Plantation," each reads "Smoke the Best - Tansill's Punch - America's Finest 5¢ Cigar," 1882 copyright, set of five, the set (ILLUS. above and previous pages) .... **1,000+**

Tray, "Banania," rectangular metal, colorful image of smiling black man wearing a fez, for a French chocolate drink, 1999 (ILLUS. below)........... **50**

Horizontal French "Banania" Tray

"Birthday Smiles" Coca-Cola Tray

Vertical French "Banania" Tray

Tray, "Banania," rectangular metal, colorful image of smiling black man wearing a fez, for a French chocolate drink, 1998 (ILLUS.) **65**

Tray, "Coca-Cola," scene of black boy & girl at birthday party, titled "Birthday Smiles," part of limited edition series based on the artwork of John Solomon Sandridge, Gadsden, Alabama, No. 2 in the series, authorized by Coca-Cola, 1996 (ILLUS.) **48**

Tray, "Coca-Cola," scene of black boy & girl seated back to back, the girl smiling w/her winnings beside her, titled "Broke 'im," part of limited edition series based on the artwork of John Solomon Sandridge, Gadsden, Alabama, No. 6 in the series, authorized by Coca-Cola, 2000 (ILLUS. below) **40**

"Broke 'im" Coca-Cola Tray

"Winning Smiles" Coca-Cola Tray

"Clean Smiles" Coca-Cola Tray

Tray, "Coca-Cola," scene of black boy & girl titled "Winning Smiles," part of limited edition series based on the artwork of John Solomon Sandridge, Gadsden, Alabama, No. 1 of 350, authorized by Coca-Cola, 1994 (ILLUS.) **45**

Tray, "Coca-Cola," scene of black boy standing holding an electric razor behind black man seated on an organ stool, titled "Clean Smiles," part of limited edition series based on the artwork of John Solomon Sandridge, Gadsden, Alabama, authorized by Coca-Cola, 1997 (ILLUS.) **45**

Tray, "Coca-Cola," scene of black boy wearing roller skates titled "Summer Smiles," part of limited edition series based on the artwork of John Solomon Sandridge, Gadsden, Alabama, No. 5 in the series, authorized by Coca-Cola, 1999 (ILLUS. below) **45**

"Summer Smiles" Coca-Cola Tray

"Tee Off" Coca-Cola Tray

Tray, "Coca-Cola," scene of black man & his son & daughter w/golf clubs, titled "Tee Off," part of limited edition series based on the artwork of John Solomon Sandridge, Gadsden, Alabama, authorized by Coca-Cola, 2001 (ILLUS.) **40**

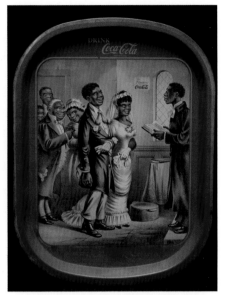

Coca-Cola Tray with Wedding Scene

Tray, "Coca-Cola," scene of "Sambo's Wedding," part of a series featuring a black couple based on drawings produced in 1916, ca. 1980 (ILLUS.) **150**

Coca-Cola Tray with Courtship Scene

Tray, "Coca-Cola," scene of "Sambo's Courtship," part of a series featuring a black couple based on drawings produced in 1916, ca. 1980 (ILLUS.) **150**

"Last Drip" Coca-Cola Tray

Tray, "Coca-Cola," scene of young black boy getting the last drop from a bottle, titled "Last Drip," part of limited edition series based on the artwork of John Solomon Sandridge, Gadsden, Alabama, No. 3 in the series, authorized by Coca-Cola, 1996 (ILLUS.)......... **40**

Large Grouping of Gold Dust Washing Powder Boxes

Washing powder box, "Fairbanks Gold Dust Washing Powder," cardboard, 4 oz. size (ILLUS. on page 35 far left with other Gold Dust containers) ... **125**

Washing powder box, "Fairbanks Gold Dust Washing Powder," cardboard, 8 oz. size (ILLUS. on page 35 far right with other Gold Dust containers) **200**

Washing powder boxes, "Fairbanks Gold Dust Washing Powder," cardboard, various sizes & ages, each featuring the Gold Dust Twins logo (ILLUS. of a large group above) . **125-250**

CANS & CONTAINERS

Early Aunt Jemima Cooking Oil Tin

Aunt Jemima Cooking & Salad Oil - Pure Corn Oil, 5 gal. tin, upright rectangular form, large color image of Aunt Jemima on red background, 1920s, some wear, 14" h. (ILLUS.) **700**

Rare Aunt Jemima Cooking Oil Tin

Aunt Jemima Cooking & Salad Oil - Pure Corn Oil, 5 gal. tin, upright rectangular form, large color image of Aunt Jemima on yellow background, 1920s, some wear, 14" h. (ILLUS.) **750**

Aunt Jemima's Sugar Butter 1 1/2 lb. can **350**

Rare Aunt Minerva Coffee Can

Aunt Minerva Coffee 3 lb. can, head of Mammy pictured, S & D Coffee Co., Concord, North Carolina, ca. 1920s, rare, 7 1/2" h. (ILLUS.) **800**

B&W Tobacco Cigar tin, lithograph of three black children, 7" h. **150**

Bergamot Hair Conditioner - Beauty Hair Dressing jar, cylindrical glass jar w/twist-off metal lid, Clayton, North Carolina, 11 oz. size, ca. 1950s (ILLUS. of lid below & side label top of next column).......................... **95**

View of a Bergamot Hair Conditioner Jar

View of a Bergamot Hair Conditioner Jar

Bill Robinson Hair Dressing tin, oblong printed metal w/snap-on lid, image of Bill Robinson dancing on the front, by Burton Brothers Co., Richmond, Virginia, ca. 1940s, 1 oz. size (ILLUS. on the right, below) **75**

Two "Bill Robinson Hair Dressing" Tins

Bill Robinson Hair Dressing tin, oblong printed metal w/snap-on lid, image of Bill Robinson dancing on the front, by Burton Brothers Co., Richmond, Virginia, ca. 1940s, 4 oz. size (ILLUS. above on the left) ... **125**

Bixby's Satinola Shoe Polish can, black shoeshine man.......................... **100**

Brown Beauty Tobacco square can, E. & W. Anstie, Ltd., Aunt Jemima-type figure pictured...................... **350-450**

Two Diamond Matches Tins

Rare Early Burnt Cork Make-up Tin

Famous Amos Butterscotch Chip Tin

Burnt Cork - For Negro Make-Up tin, short round printed metal tin, Charles Meyer Mfg. Co., New York, New York, early 20th c. (ILLUS.) ... **1,200**

Diamond Matches tin, long narrow metal form, brassy gold background printed w/a scene of a black family, early 20th c., 1 1/2 x 4 1/2" (ILLUS. on left with other Diamond tin top of page)........ **350**

Diamond Matches tin, long narrow metal form, white background printed w/a scene of a black family, early 20th c., 1 1/2 x 4 1/2" (ILLUS. on right with other Diamond tin top of page) **350**

Dinah Black Enamel Paint can, features Dinah walking around the can **100-150**

Dixie Brand Jumbo Salted Peanuts, 10 lb. can, The Kelly Peanut Co., Boston, Massachusetts, early 20th c., 9" h. ... **500**

Excelsior Varnish Works tin, turpentine for black asphalt, features a black man .... **100+**

Famous Amos Butterscotch Chip Cookies, round 32 oz. tin, cartoon bust portrait of Amos wearing Scottish outfit on the lid (ILLUS.) **100**

Famous Amos 10th Anniversary Tin

Famous Amos Chocolate Chip Cookies, round 15 oz. tin, 10th Anniversary special edition (ILLUS. previous page) **100**

Famous Amos Cookies 24 oz. Tin

Famous Amos Cookies, round 24 oz. tin, cover photo of huge cookie held up by Amos, includes brief history of the founding of the company in 1975 (ILLUS.) **95**

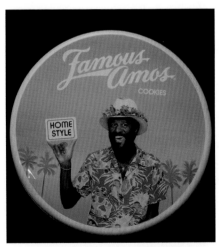

Cookie Tin with Wally Amos Photo

Famous Amos Cookies, round 24 oz. tin, lid w/photo of Wally Amos wearing tropical shirt, 1976 (ILLUS.) **95**

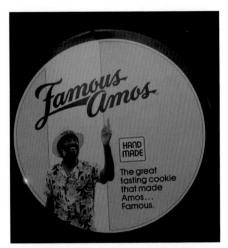

Famous Amos Variety Cookies Tin

Famous Amos Cookies, round tin, special variety selection, 1979 (ILLUS.)... **100**

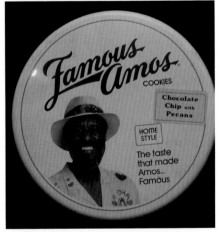

Home Style Chocolate Chip Cookie Tin

Famous Amos Home Style Chocolate Chip with Pecans Cookies, round 15 oz. tin, bust photo of Wally Amos on lid (ILLUS.) **100**

Grady's Liquid Scouree Polish can, cylindrical w/domed top & screw-on cap, illustrated w/image of black man polishing a metal ewer, The Grady Manufacturing Co., New York, New York, ca. 1880s (ILLUS. next page) **225**

Early Grady's Liquid Scouree Polish Can

Ideal Blend Coffee tin, featuring black Mammy, Jones & Co., New York **200**

"Joe Louis Hair Pomade" Tin

Joe Louis Hair Pomade tin, low round printed metal tin, photo of Joe Louis on cover, Joe Louis Products Co., Chicago, ca. 1950s (ILLUS.) **200**

Jumbo Dixie Peanut pail, black man w/peanut in his mouth, Kelly Peanut Co., Boston, Massachusetts, large, approximately 15" h.................... **600-800**

Lipton (Thomas J.) Tea 3 lb. can, features black woman picking tea leaves... **100-150**

Luter's Lard 8 lb. can, Mammy holding large spatula, various sizes **350**

Luzianne Coffee tin, featuring Mammy in oval vignette shown drinking from saucer, 3 lb. size, very early variation dated 1928, sold w/cup & saucer inside, Wm. B. Reily & Co., 7 1/2" h. (ILLUS. bottom row, second from right with other Luzianne cans, bottom of page) **300**

Luzianne Coffee tin, featuring Mammy pouring coffee, 1 lb. size, white background, ca. 1940s, 5 1/4" h. (ILLUS. top row, top second from left with other Luzianne cans, below) **65**

Luzianne Coffee tin, featuring Mammy pouring coffee, 1 lb. size, white background w/"35¢ Off" notice on front, ca. 1940s, 5 1/4" h. (ILLUS. top row, far left with other Luzianne cans, below)... **65**

Luzianne Coffee tin, featuring Mammy pouring coffee, 2 lb. size, white background & paper label w/"20¢ Off " coupon offer, ca. 1930s, 6 1/2" h. (ILLUS. top row, third from left with other Luzianne cans, below)..... **95**

Grouping of Luzianne Coffee and other Containers

Rare Mackintosh's Rag-Time Candy Tin

Luzianne Coffee tin, featuring Mammy serving coffee, 1 lb. size, red background w/"5¢ Off Introductory Offer," ca. 1940s, 5 1/4" h. (ILLUS. top row, bottom second from left with other Luzianne cans previous page) **95**

Luzianne Coffee tin, featuring Mammy serving coffee, 2 lb. size, red paper label on red background, ca. 1940s, 6 1/2" h. (ILLUS. top row, second from right with other Luzianne cans previous page) **140**

Luzianne Coffee tin, featuring Mammy serving coffee, 3 lb. size, red background, ca. 1940s, 7 1/4" h. (ILLUS. top row, far right with other Luzianne cans previous page) **140**

Luzianne Coffee tin, featuring Mammy serving coffee, 3 lb. size, red background, young looking Mammy, Wm. B. Reily & Co., ca. 1950s, 7 1/4" h. (ILLUS. bottom row, far right with other Luzianne cans previous page) **125**

Luzianne Coffee tin, featuring Mammy serving coffee, 3 lb. size, white background, young looking Mammy, sold w/cup & saucer inside, Wm. B. Reily & Co., ca. 1950s, 7 1/4" h. (ILLUS. bottom row, second from left with other Luzianne cans previous page) **125**

Mackintosh's Rag-Time Candy tin, black man & woman doing the Cake Walk, Halifax, England (ILLUS. above) **650-700**

Madam Walker's Skin Brightener Tin

Madam C.J. Walker's Skin Brightener tin, cylindrical metal tin, early 20th c. (ILLUS. above and part of kit page 13) **250**

Madam Walker's Hair Grower Tin

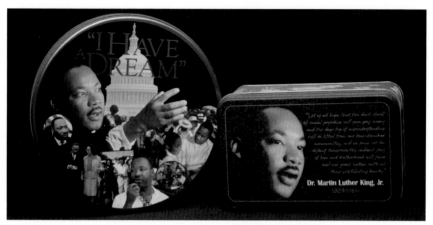

Two Martin Luther King Jr. Commemorative Tins

Madam C.J. Walker's Wonderful Hair Grower tin, cylindrical metal tin, photo of a pretty long-haired black woman on the lid, early 20th c. (ILLUS. previous page and part of kit page 13) **200**

Madam Walker's Temple Salve Tin

Madam C.J. Walker's Wonderful Temple Salve tin, cylindrical metal tin, early 20th c. (ILLUS. and part of kit page 13)... **250**

Mammy's Favorite Brand Coffee 4 lb. can, features black Mammy holding tray w/pot of coffee & cups, C.D. Kenny, Baltimore, Maryland **350**

Martin Luther King Jr. commemorative tin, rectangular, close-up of Dr. King beside one of his quotes, photo by Flip Schulke, produced by Intellectual Properties Management, Inc., Atlanta, Georgia (ILLUS. right with other tin, top of page) **35**

Martin Luther King Jr. commemorative tin, round, top printed w/various photo portraits of Dr. King, photos by Flip Schulke, produced by Intellectual Properties Management, Inc., Atlanta, Georgia (ILLUS. left with other tin above) **35**

Mazannattee Tea can, colorful lithographed label of three black boys drinking tea out of cups **800-1,000**

"Mildred's Scalp Ointment" Jar

Mildred's Scalp Ointment jar, cylindrical jar w/twist-off metal lid, paper label w/picture of black woman, San Francisco, California, ca. 1940s (ILLUS.).................................... **75**

Negertjes Cigar tin, rectangular, featuring lithographed black & white photo label of two black children smoking cigars, Europe, ca. 1940s, 4 1/2 x 7 1/4" (ILLUS. next page) **350**

Negertjes Cigar Tin

Negri Polish Cylindrical Can

Negri metal polishing cream can, cylindrical tin w/bust portrait of a smiling black man, label at bottom front in French & German, ca. 1940s (ILLUS., previous column) **150**

Negro Head Brand Oysters 10 oz. can, features black man & plate of oysters, distributed by Aughinbaugh Canning Co., Biloxi, Mississippi, ca. 1940, 5" h. (ILLUS. left with shrimp can, below) **500**

Negro Head Brand Oysters 8 oz. can, features black man holding oyster fork, distributed by Aughinbaugh Canning Co., Biloxi, Mississippi, ca. 1940, 3" h. **200**

Negro Head Brand Shrimp 10 oz. can, features black man & plate of shrimp, distributed by Aughinbaugh Canning Co., Biloxi, Mississippi, ca. 1940, 5" h. (ILLUS. below right with oysters can) **500**

Negro Head Oyster & Shrimp Cans

Rare Nigger Head Oysters Can & Labeled Box

Early Nigger Hair Tobacco Pail

Nigger Hair Smoking Tobacco pail, printed metal w/fitted cap & wire bail handle, wording & image of native head on a dark orange background, original paper liner, early 20th c., 5 1/4" d., 6 1/2" h. (ILLUS.) **575**

Nigger Head Oysters can, 10 oz. cylindrical w/paper label featuring grotesque profile of black man about to eat an oyster, w/original shipping box w/matching label, distributed by Aughinbaugh Canning Co., Biloxi, Mississippi, early 20th c., can 5" h., can w/label, $1,000; complete w/box, the set (ILLUS. top of page) **1,500**

Nigger Head Tomatoes can, featuring grotesque profile of black man about to eat tomato **800-1,000**

Old Black Joe Grease 1 lb. can, John Hancock Oil Co. **150**

Old Black Joe Grease 10 lb. can, John Hancock Oil Co **350**

Picaninny Brand Jumbo Salted Peanuts, 10 lb. can, yellow ground w/large red band w/wording enclosing scene of small black child in the center, F.M. Hoyt & Co., Amesbury, Massachusetts, early 20th c., 9" h. (ILLUS. bottom row, far left with the Luzianne Coffee cans, page 54) **500**

Pickaninny Brand Peanut Butter 1 lb. tin, rare size **500-700**

Pickaninny Brand Peanut Butter tin, Canco, 3 1/2 x 3 3/4" **250-350**

Queen Hair Dressing Tin

Queen Hair Dressing tin, printed metal w/snap-on lid, small picture of woman on front, Newbro Mfg. Co., Atlanta, Georgia, early 20th c., some wear (ILLUS.) **75**

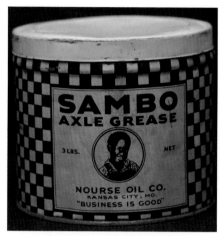

Sambo Axle Grease 3 lb. Can

Sambo Axle Grease 3 lb. can, black boy w/big grin, Nourse Oil Co., Kansas City, Missouri (ILLUS.) **200**

Southern Biscuit Co. tin, features black butler, Richmond, Virginia ...... **100+**

Spriggs Black and Tan Cigars can, upright square shape w/pry-off lid, two small illustrations of black children on the front, A.E. Spriggs, Joplin, Missouri, early 20th c. (ILLUS. right)... **250**

Sunny South Sweet Milk Chocolate Peanuts 1 lb. can, featuring colorful printed label centered by head of black woman wearing large red hat & polka dot bow, flanked by white

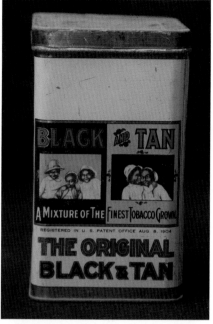

Early Spriggs Black and Tan Cigar Can

scrolls & brown candy on blue ground (ILLUS. below) **250-300**

Sweet Georgia Brown Bright Skin Cleansing Cream jar, cylindrical glass jar w/screw-on lid, paper label centered by circle enclosing heads of black woman & man, Valmor Products, Chicago, ca. 1950s (ILLUS. next page) **125**

Sunny South Sweet Milk Chocolate Peanuts Can

"Sweet Georgia Brown" Skin Cream

View of a Wavine Hair Dressing Jar

"Tuskegee Belle Hair Dressing" Tin

Tuskegee Belle Hair Dressing tin,
oblong upright printed metal tin, col-
or scene w/buildings in background
centered by round photo of young
black woman graduate, Capital
Chemical Drug Co., Montgomery,
Alabama, early 20th c. (ILLUS.).......... **250**

View of a Wavine Hair Dressing Jar

Wavine Hair Dressing jar, cylindrical
glass jar w/twist-off metal lid, wrap-
around paper label w/sketched portrait of pretty black girl w/long wavy
hair, Boyd Mfg. Co., Birmingham,
Alabama, ca. 1930s (ILLUS. of two
views) **150**

Coon-Chicken Inn Ceramic Cookie Jar

COON-CHICKEN INN ITEMS

Coon-Chicken Inn advertising card, linen-type postcard showing restaurant & location **80**

Coon-Chicken Inn bread plate, ceramic, 6 1/2" d. **200**

Coon-Chicken Inn carry-out chicken box container, featuring typical logo, 1925-50s, 7 1/4 x 11" **125**

Coon-Chicken Inn cereal bowl, ceramic **250**

Coon-Chicken Inn cigarette caddy, ceramic, w/place for cigarettes & matches **150**

Coon-Chicken Inn coffee cup & saucer, ceramic, both w/logo, the set **500**

Coon-Chicken Inn cookie tin, lithographed metal, in the shape of an early trolley car-style diner, by Accouterments, Seattle, Washington, made in China, 2003, 4 x 8" (ILLUS. above) **125**

Coon-Chicken Inn demitasse cup & saucer, ceramic, the set **550-650**

Coon-Chicken Inn dessert or custard cup, round, ceramic **225**

Coon-Chicken Inn dinner plate, caricature bellhop logo in center, 9 1/2" d. (ILLUS.) **250-300**

Coon-Chicken Inn Dinner Plate

Rare Coon-Chicken Inn Cloth Doll

Coon-Chicken Inn doll, stuffed canvas-like cloth, hand-sewn, wearing red felt outfit, ca. 1940s, very rare, 28" h. (ILLUS. previous page).......... **1,500**

Coon-Chicken Inn flatware set: spoon, fork & knife; metal, the set **75-100**

Coon-Chicken Inn French fry bag, very scarce **300-400**

Coon-Chicken Inn matchbook, w/logo on each match..................... **70-80**

Coon-Chicken Inn matchbook, w/plain matches **35-40**

Coon-Chicken Inn Die-Cut Menu

Coon-Chicken Inn menu, grotesque caricature head w/large red smiling lips revealing name of restaurant written across teeth, 1925-50s, 9 x 12 3/4" (ILLUS.)......................... **125+**

Coon-Chicken Inn menu, same as above but smallest size, children's menu, 4 3/4" **100**

Coon-Chicken Inn menu, same as above only smaller size, 8"................. **150**

Coon-Chicken Inn napkin, large dinner size... **25-30**

Coon-Chicken Inn placemat, all restaurant locations noted on map, 10 1/2 x 14 1/2" **60-80**

Coon-Chicken Inn platter, ceramic, oval serving-type, flat w/logo in center, 12 1/2" l. **450**

Coon-Chicken Inn receipt book **100**

Coon-Chicken Inn "Reserved" card, 4 1/4 x 5 1/2" **50**

Coon-Chicken Inn salad bowl, ceramic, 8 1/2" d. **250**

Coon-Chicken Inn soup bowl, ceramic... **250**

Coon-Chicken Inn steak plate, ceramic, contoured oval-shape w/logo in center, 11" l. .... **400+**

Coon-Chicken Inn straw holder **450**

Coon-Chicken Inn toothpick holder, ceramic... **150**

Coon-Chicken Inn toothpick holder, metal.. **250**

— Chapter 2 —
BANKS

Dinah & Two "Jolly Nigger" Banks

Mechanical

Numbers at the end of entries refer to listings in the book Penny Lane - A History of Antique Mechanical Toy Banks, by Al Davidson (Long's Americana, 1987).

Bad Accident Mechanical Bank

Bad Accident - 9 - man riding in cart pulled by donkey w/boy hiding behind cattail plant, J. & E. Stevens, multicolored, overpaint on driver, cart & boy, PL 20 (ILLUS.).. **$1,500-2,000**

Bamboula, French version of "Jolly Nigger," on back of bank below name "Depose," ca. 1890-1900 (PL 21)... **2,500-3,000**

Boys Stealing Watermelons - 22 - doghouse w/dog, two boys stealing watermelons, Kyser & Rex, multicolored, ca. 1885-95, 7" w. (PL 53).. **5,000**

Cabin Bank with Black Man

Cabin - 33 - cabin w/man standing in doorway, red & black w/yellow walls, pivoting man kicks coin through roof, J. & E. Stevens, PL 93 (ILLUS.) **2,415**

Darktown Battery Mechanical Bank

Aluminum "Jolly Nigger" and Dinah Mechanical Banks

Darktown Battery - 56 - three black baseball figures - pitcher, catcher, & batter - multicolored, known in rarer white player version, J. & E. Stevens, ca. 1888, probable repaint of pitcher, 9 3/4", PL 146 (ILLUS. bottom of previous page) **1,265**

Darky and Watermelon (Football Bank) - 92 - place coin in the football & pull figure's right leg back until it locks; press lever on figure's back & he kicks the football, dropping coin into bank, J. & E. Stevens, ca. 1888, PL 147, extremely rare, auction price in 1998 .... **354,500**

Dinah - bust of black woman, aluminum, places coin in mouth, "Dinah" cast on back, eyes roll back as arm moves, short-sleeved red dress, attributed to England, ca. 1920s, PL 154 (ILLUS. top of page right with "Jolly Nigger" bank with moveable ears) **350**

Dinah Mechanical Bank

Dinah - 58 - bust of black woman, places coin in mouth, "Dinah" cast on back, short-sleeved yellow dress, overpaint to dress, PL 153 (ILLUS. top right column) **500-1,000**

(I) Always Did 'Spise a Mule - 4 - boy on bench facing mule, red version, rarer white plus white version known, by J. E. Stevens Co., coin trap missing, 10" w., PL 250 (ILLUS. right) **800-1,000**

*"Always Did 'Spise a Mule"
Bank Variation*

"Always Did 'Spise a Mule" Bank

"Jolly Nigger" Bank with Top Hat

Little Joe Bank, aluminum, bust w/extended right hand, wearing small white hat, "Little Joe Bank" cast into back, attributed to John Harper & Co., England (PL 305)............. **500-1,000**

Mammy & Child - 155 - mammy feeding child laying across lap, multicolored, Kyser & Rex, 1884 (PL 318) .. **8,500**

J.E. Stevens "Jolly Nigger Bank"

(l) Always Did 'Spise a Mule - 5 - black jockey riding mule, PL 251 (ILLUS. top)............................ **700-1,200**

"Jolly Nigger Bank" - 132 - red shirt, moving arm, tongue & rolling eyes, J. & E. Stevens, patented on March 14, 1882, 1880s-1930s, many variations, PL 275 (ILLUS. above)......... **1,000**

"Jolly Nigger Bank" (High Hat) - 135 - black man wearing red coat & red top hat, eyes roll & tongue moves, John Harper & Co., England, PL 277 (ILLUS. next column)............... **1,200**

Jolly Nigger (S. & M.) - cast iron, no hat, blue tie, label marked "Beacon Products, S & M Ltd." on back, Sydenham & McOustra, England, 5 1/2" h. (PL 273)............................ **100+**

Jolly Nigger (Starkie Patent) - 137 - aluminum, moves ears, no hat, red coat, white collar, blue tie, by Starkie, England, ca. 1920, 6 1/2" h., PL 271 (ILLUS. left with Dinah bank, previous page) **350**

Stump Speaker Mechanical Bank

Stump Speaker - 222 - standing Black figure w/carpetbag, w/moving arm & opening mouth & carpetbag, multicolored, Shepard Hardware, ca. 1896, top & areas of base repainted, minor in-painting on figure, PL 453 (ILLUS.) **800-1,200**

Uncle Remus - 230 - cast iron, figure holding chicken in doorway of chicken coop w/policeman holding stick outside, Kyser & Rex Co. or Mechanical Novelty Works, if in near mint condition, PL 492 (ILLUS. previous page).................................... **3,500-4,500**

Still

Numbers at end of listings from The Penny Bank Book - Collecting Still Banks, by Andy and Susan Moore (Schiffer Publishing, Ltd., 1984). An asterisk (*) indicates a bank that has been reproduced.

Black Boy - Two-Faced Black Boy (Negro Toy Bank) - 83 - cast iron, A.C. Williams Co., 1901-19, 4 1/8" h. (W. 43)................................. **250**

Black Man - Darkey (Sharecropper) - 173 - cast iron, w/toes visible on one foot, black paint w/red trim, A.C. Williams Co., 1901, 5 1/2" h. (W. 18)........ **250**

Black Man with Suitcase Bank

Black man w/suitcase, cast iron, kneeling figure wearing red coat, white shirt, black tie & white brimmed hat, his arms crossed in front of him & leaning on a suitcase, original paint fair, 7 3/4" h. (ILLUS.).... **201**

Black Woman - Mammy with Basket - 175 - white metal, key-locked trap, clothes basket under right arm, America, 5 1/4" h. .... **3,000+**

*Black Woman - Mammy with Hands on Hips - 176 - cast iron, blue kerchief w/white dots, red blouse & white scarf, long white dress, Hubley Mfg. Co., 1914-46, 5 1/4" h. (W. 20).. **125**

*Black Woman - (Mammy with Spoon) - 168 - cast iron, blue, red & silver paint, A.C. Williams Co., 1905-30, 5 7/8" h. (W. 17).................. **350**

Black Woman - (Mammy with Spoon) - 169 - cast iron, slot between legs, American-made, 5 7/8" h. **363**

Man on Cotton Bale (Coon Bank) - 37 - cast iron, U.S. Hardware Co., 1898, 4" w., 4 7/8" h. (W. 37) .... **3,000+**

Tin

Numbers at end are from the Penny Lane book by Davidson.

Cross Legged Minstrel, tin mechanical, standing black minstrel w/legs crossed, wearing a colorful outfit, a top hat held in one raised arm, coin inserted in chest, lever pressed on lower left side, coin enters back & arm waves the hat, based on an English patent, apparently manufactured in Germany, ca. 1910, scarce (PL 142)...................................... **2,000+**

Minstrel - tin mechanical, arched pedestal w/face of a black man at top, press lever at front & he sticks his tongue out to receive the coin, then rolls his eyes, Saalheimer & Strauss, Germany, ca. 1930 (PL 328) .... **250+**

— Chapter 3 —
COOKIE JARS & RELATED CONTAINERS

A Large Collection of Cookie Jars

A Company of 2 Black Girl Cookie Jar

A Company of 2, black girl w/actual braided hair, David Brdecko, modern (ILLUS.) **$450**

Sister Chubby Cheeks Cookie Jar

A Company of 2, Sister Chubby Cheeks, marked "A Company of 2 - David Brdecko Original Limited Edition #1," modern (ILLUS.)................... **400**

A Little Company Bella Cookie Jar

A Little Company, Bella, contemporary, Santa Fe, New Mexico (ILLUS.) **350**

A Little Company Edmund Cookie Jar

A Little Company, Edmund, contemporary, Santa Fe, New Mexico (ILLUS.) **450-600**

A Little Company, Josephine Baker bust, based on 1929 photograph, contemporary, Santa Fe, New Mexico (ILLUS. top right column) ... **800-1,000**

A Little Company, Rosa Parks, bust portrait of Civil Rights pioneer, commissioned by Rogers Lewis, produced by A Little Company, 1999, 13 1/2" h. (ILLUS. of front & back right bottom two photos) **350**

A Little Company Josephine Baker Jar

Front & Back of Rosa Parks Cookie Jar

Abingdon Mammy, apron w/floral design, marked "U.S.A.," 1940s, 10" h... **350-450**

Artistic Pottery Chef, solid color, came in a variety of colors, brown is rarest, looks like National Silver Co. model, white................................ **300-400**

Artistic Pottery Chef, solid color, came in a variety of colors, brown is rarest, looks like National Silver Co. model, aqua **400-500**

Artistic Pottery Chef, solid color, came in a variety of colors, brown is rarest, looks like National Silver Co. model, pink **400-500**

Artistic Pottery Chef, solid color, came in a variety of colors, brown is rarest, looks like National Silver Co. model, brown **600-800**

Artistic Pottery Mammy, solid color, came in a variety of colors, brown is rarest, looks like National Silver Co. Mammy, white............................. **300-400**

Artistic Pottery Mammy, solid color, came in a variety of colors, brown is rarest, looks like National Silver Co. Mammy, aqua **400-500**

Artistic Pottery Mammy, solid color, came in a variety of colors, brown is rarest, looks like National Silver Co. Mammy, pink **400-500**

Artistic Pottery Mammy, solid color, came in a variety of colors, brown is rarest, looks like National Silver Co. Mammy, brown **600-800**

"Aunt Jemima," ceramic, polka dot dress, plaid kerchief & striped apron w/wording, artist-made, Wolfe Studio, Michigan, modern (ILLUS. top right column) **225**

Aunt Jemima, hard plastic, premium offered by Quaker Oats Co., made by F & F Mold and Die Works, Dayton, Ohio, 1951 .... **450-600**

Aunt Jemima, soft plastic premium offered by Quaker Oats Co. **250-350**

Aunt Susan, large rounded figure of a black Mammy w/hands on her waist, North Dakota School of Mines, very rare (ILLUS. right column) .... **4,000+**

Wolfe Studio "Aunt Jemima" Jar

Very Rare Aunt Susan Cookie Jar

Basket Handle Butler Figure, "The Herringbone Butler," mate to Mammy w/elongated body, Japan, 8 1/2" h. (ILLUS. next page) **3,000**

Basket Handle Butler Figure, hands clasped, wearing a black tuxedo w/blue pants, marked "Japan," 10" h. **1,000-1,250**

Basket Handle Mammy Figure Containers

Rare Elongated Body Butler Jar

Rare Elongated Body Mammy Jar

Basket Handle Butler Figure biscuit jar, hands clasped, same as cookie jar, black jacket, green pants, 7" h. **..... 800-1,000**

Basket Handle Mammy Figure, elongated body, mate to Butler w/herringbone trousers, marked "Japan," very rare, 8 1/2" h. (ILLUS. bottom right).. **2,500**

Basket Handle Mammy Figure, plaid dress, feet showing, hands clasped at waist, mate to Butler cookie jar, marked "Japan," 10" h. **1,000-1,250**

Basket Handle Mammy Figure, plaid dress w/polka dots on sleeve, no feet showing, Japan, 10" h. **800-1,000**

Basket Handle Mammy Figure, polka dot dress w/plaid apron, Japan, 10" h. (ILLUS. center back with other Mammy wearing polka dot dress pieces, top of previous page).. **1,200-1,500**

Basket Handle Mammy Figure, Weller lookalike, Maruhon Ware, Japan................................... **2,500-3,000**

Basket Handle Mammy Figure biscuit jar, matches Mammy wearing plaid dress w/polka dot sleeves, Japan, 7" h..................................... **700-900**

Basket Handle Mammy Figure biscuit jar, polka dot dress w/plaid apron, Japan, 7" h. (ILLUS. right with other Mammy wearing polka dot dress pieces, top of previous page)..... **800-1,000**

Basket Handle Mammy Figure biscuit jar, plaid dress, feet showing, hands clasped at waist, mate to Mammy Figure cookie jar, marked "Japan," 7" h. **800-1,000**

Basket Handle Mammy Figure creamer & covered sugar bowl, polka dot dress w/plaid apron, Japan, pr. (ILLUS. left with other Mammy wearing polka dot dress pieces top of previous page) **650**

Basket Handle Mammy Head, figural yellow rose finial on the cover, yellow collar, Maruhon Ware, Japan (ILLUS.) **1,500-2,000**

Basket Handle Mammy w/Yellow Rose

Basket Handle Mammy Head, smiling brown face w/large eyes, wearing red kerchief, wicker bail handle, unmarked (ILLUS. below center with other Basket Handle pieces) **1,200**

Basket Handle Mammy Head biscuit jar, smiling brown face w/large eyes, wearing red kerchief, wicker bail handle, unmarked (ILLUS. below right with other Basket Handle pieces)... **800**

Basket Handle Mammy Head salt & pepper shakers, small teapot-shaped heads w/wire bail handles, unmarked, pr. (ILLUS. below left with other Basket Handle pieces).... **50-75**

Basket Handle Mammy Head Containers

Black Fireman Head Containers

Black Fireman biscuit jar, smiling head w/mustache & red helmet complete w/badge, wire bail handle, Japan (ILLUS. above far right w/other Black Fireman pieces) .. **400-500**

Black Fireman cookie jar, smiling head w/mustache & red helmet complete w/badge, wire bail handle, Japan (ILLUS. above second from right w/other Black Fireman pieces) **500-700**

Black Fireman salt & pepper shakers, smiling head w/mustache & red helmet complete w/badge, wire bail handle, Japan, pr. (ILLUS. above page far left w/other Black Fireman pieces) **150**

Black Fireman teapot, smiling head w/mustache & red helmet complete w/badge, wire bail handle, Japan (ILLUS. above third from right w/other Black Fireman pieces) **450**

Black Maid, ceramic, one-of-a-kind in green dress & white apron trimmed in lace, holding a pie, heavy pottery, similar to Brayton Laguna maid jar (ILLUS. right) **1,000**

Brayton - Laguna Mammy, blue dress & white apron bordered w/a zig-zag colored pattern & a red bandanna, Laguna Beach, California, 12 5/8" h. **1,000-1,200**

Rare Black Maid Cookie Jar

Brayton - Laguna Mammy, burgundy dress & white apron bordered w/a zig-zag colored pattern & a red bandanna, Laguna Beach, California, 12 5/8" h. **1,000-1,200**

Brayton - Laguna Mammy, green dress & white apron bordered w/a zig-zag colored pattern & a red bandanna, Laguna Beach, California, 12 5/8" h. (ILLUS. top of next page) **1,000-1,200**

Brayton-Laguna Mammy in Green

Rare Brayton-Laguna Maid Cookie Jar

Brayton - Laguna Mammy, mustard yellow dress & white apron bordered w/a zig-zag colored pattern & a red bandanna, Laguna Beach, California, 12 5/8" h. **1,500**

Brayton - Laguna Mammy, red dress & white apron bordered w/a zig-zag colored pattern & a red bandanna, Laguna Beach, California, 12 5/8" h. .... **600-800+**

Brayton - Laguna Mammy, yellow dress & white apron bordered w/a zig-zag colored pattern & a red bandanna, Laguna Beach, California, 12 5/8" h. **800-1,000**

Brayton - Laguna Maid, rare piece w/black dress & white apron, Laguna Beach, California .... **3,500+**

Brayton - Laguna Maid, rarest version wearing blue dress, Laguna Beach, California (ILLUS. top right column) **8,500+**

Chef, resembles National Silver Co. Chef, 1930s, unmarked **250**

Cream of Wheat Chef, biscuit jar size, 8" h. (ILLUS. top of next page right with Cream of Wheat cookie jar)....................................... **1,000-1,200**

Cream of Wheat Chef, cookie jar, 9 1/2" h. (ILLUS. top of next page with biscuit jar bottom previous page)..................................... **1,200-1,500**

Enesco Chef, Chef holding a large red spoon, Japan, 7" h. (ILLUS. next page right with other Enesco pieces).. **1,200**

Enesco Mammy, Mammy holding a large red spoon, Japan, 7" h. (ILLUS. bottom of next page left with other Enesco pieces) **1,500-1,700**

Enesco salt & pepper shakers, figures of Mammy & Chef, pr. (ILLUS. bottom of next page center with other Enesco pieces)............................... **65+**

Fall Creek Mammy, red & white, hands clasped in front, large apron, Fall Creek Ceramic Co., 10" h..... **250-350**

Fall Creek Mammy, yellow & white, hands clasped in front, large apron, Fall Creek Ceramic Co., 10" h..... **250-350**

Fitz & Floyd "Rio Rita," black Carmen Miranda-type figure w/red parrot perched on her shoulder & a hat w/fruit, contemporary **350-450**

Gilner Mammy, bust only, white dress & kerchief, unmarked, 11" h. (ILLUS. page 75 with other Gilner Mammy)..................... **1,200-1,300**

Gilner Mammy, bust only, yellow dress & kerchief, unmarked, 11" h. (ILLUS. page 75 left) **1,200-1,300**

Cream of Wheat Chef Jars & Sign

Enesco Cookie Jars & Shakers

Two Gilner Mammy Cookie Jars

Three Rare "Googly-eyed" Cookie Jars

"Gone With the Wind" Mammy, glazed version, Hamilton Gifts, 1990 (ILLUS.) **400-450**

"Gone With the Wind" Mammy, original jar unglazed, Hamilton Gifts, 1990 .... **600-700**

"Googly-eyed" Mammy, ceramic, wearing kerchief, wrapped bail handle, rare, 8" h. (ILLUS. center with other "googly-eyed" cookie jars) **1,000**

Googly-eyed Mammy biscuit jar, red polka dot bandanna, head only, w/basketweave handles, matches cookie jar, rare, 6" h. **800-900**

Googly-eyed Mammy cookie jar, red polka dot bandanna, head only, w/basketweave handles, rare, 8" h. **1,200**

"Googly-eyed" Man, ceramic, wearing a beret forming the cover, rare, 7 1/4" h. (ILLUS. left with other "googly-eyed" cookie jars) **1,200**

"Googly-eyed" Man, ceramic, wearing straw-style boater hat forming the cover, bail handle w/wire grip, rare, 8" h. (ILLUS. right with other "googly-eyed" cookie jars) **2,500**

Googly-eyed man, head only, yellow hat, red polka dot bow tie, w/basketweave handles, marked "Japan," very rare, 6 1/2" h. .... **4,000+**

Kathy Wolfe Studio Cookie Jars

Italian-made Mammy Biscuit Jar

Indian woman, black skin, wearing an Indian necklace, unmarked, 13" h. **350-450**

Italian Mammy biscuit jar, ceramic, full-figure wearing a flowered long dress, blouse & kerchief, hands at her front, marked "Made in Italy - #7826," ca. 1950s, 8" h. (ILLUS. above) **800**

Japan Mammy, polka dot green dress w/blue border, unmarked, 1940s. **350-400**

Jug-form, decorated w/scene of little black girl playing w/cookie jar & little dog, marked "Canuck Potter, St. John. N.B. Canada" .... **700+**

Kathy Wolfe Studio, ceramic, Maid, figure wearing apron marked "BBQ," 1995 (ILLUS. above left with Pretty Lady cookie jar) **225**

Kathy Wolfe Studio, Pretty Lady, figure of black woman wearing a fancy ruffled floral dress & hat, 1995 (ILLUS. above right with Kathy Wolfe Maid cookie jar) **225**

Luzianne Mammy, full-figure, marked "U.S.A." **800-1,000**

Mammy, resembles National Silver Co. Mammy, unmarked, 1930s **250**

Mammy candy jar, a full-figured laughing Mammy, white dress w/red trim & kerchief, 6" h. (ILLUS. top of next page) **300-600**

Mammy McCoy lookalike with blonde hair, "Cookies" embossed along bottom of her dress, rare (ILLUS. top right next page) .. **1,200-1,300**

Figural Mammy Candy Jar

Maruhon Ware Mammy, basket-handled full-figure jar, copy of Weller Mammy jar, blue kerchief & red kerchief variations, very rare, each (ILLUS. of two below) **2,500**

McCoy cylinder, h.p. bust of a black boy signed "V.H.," jar ca. 1946-54 (ILLUS. top of next page)............ **400-500**

McCoy Mammy, aqua dress **600**

McCoy Lookalike Mammy Cookie Jar

McCoy Mammy, Cauliflower Mammy, marked "U.S.A.," 1939 (ILLUS. next page) **500-600**

McCoy Mammy, jar w/inscription around the bottom of dress reading "Cookies sure got date vitamin A," very rare, yellow dress .... **4,000+**

Rare Maruhon Ware Mammy Jars

McCoy Cylinder Cookie Jar

McCoy Mammy, w/inscription around bottom of dress, aqua dress, very rare .... **4,000+**

McCoy Cauliflower Mammy Cookie Jar

McCoy Mammy, white dress, late 1940s - early 1950s, common, 11" h **125-200**

McCoy Mammy, yellow dress .... **500+**

Metlox Pottery Black Santa, full-figure complete w/sack of toys, California.................................... **600-700**

Metlox Pottery Mammy, holding mixing bowl, white dress w/blue polka dots, California, 1940s **500-600**

Metlox Pottery Mammy, holding mixing bowl, white dress w/red polka dots, California, 1940s................. **500-600**

Metlox Washtub Mammy Cookie Jar

Metlox Pottery Mammy, Washtub Mammy, unmarked, California, late 1940s (ILLUS.) **1,500**

Metlox Pottery Mammy, white dress w/yellow polka dots, California, 1940s.. **500-650**

Metlox Pottery Topsy, young pigtailed girl, white dress w/blue polka dots, California, late 1940s **400-500**

Metlox Pottery Topsy, young pigtailed girl, white dress w/no polka dots, blue apron, California, late 1940s.. **500-600**

Metlox Pottery Topsy, young pigtailed girl, white dress w/red polka dots, California, late 1940s **400-500**

Metlox Pottery Topsy, young pigtailed girl, white dress w/yellow polka dots, California, late 1940s **400-500**

Mosaic Tile Mammy, black & white dress, rarer colors **1,500-1,600**

Mosaic Tile Mammy, blue dress, common color............................. **600-700**

Mosaic Tile Mammy, blue & yellow dress, rare colors................... **1,000-1,200**

Mosaic Tile Mammy, peach & green dress, rare colors **1,000-1,200**

Mosaic Tile Mammy, tan dress, rarer color **1,800-2,000**

Mosaic Tile Mammy, yellow dress, common color **450-550**

National Silver Co. Chef, navy blue striped pants & waiter's jacket, marked "N.F.C.O.," 10 1/4" h. **250-350**

National Silver Co. Mammy, hands clasped in front, wears white & blue bandanna & green polka dot apron **350**

Rare Pearl Watermelon Mammy Jar

Pearl China Company Watermelon Mammy, figure holding a slice of watermelon up to her mouth, long white dress, rare (ILLUS.) .... **3,000+**

New Rose Watermelon Boy & Girl

New Rose Collection Watermelon Boy, seated figure, blue pants & cap, by Rose Saxby, Warren, Illinois, contemporary (ILLUS. left with girl) .... **250+**

New Rose Collection Watermelon Girl, seated figure, lavender dress w/gold bows, by Rose Saxby, Warren, Illinois, contemporary (ILLUS. right with boy) .... **250+**

Omnibus Japan Mandy - round, figure of Mandy holding a basket of flowers .... **300+**

Pearl China Company Chef, 10 3/4" h...................................... **400-600**

Pearl China Company Mammy, 10 3/4" h... **550+**

Plaid Apron Mammy Cookie Jar

Plaid Apron Mammy, holding spoon, Japan (ILLUS.) .... **400+**

Polka Dot Mammy Cookie Jar

Polka Dot Mammy, all yellow w/burgundy polka dots, unknown origin, 12 1/2" h. (ILLUS.) .... **850+**

Renita Pines Beloved Belindy Jar

Renita Pines Beloved Belindy, contemporary, Oakland, California (ILLUS.) **850**

Rick Wisecarver - Mammy at the stove, 1990s **400-500**

Rick Wisecarver - Mammy bust, black woman w/lace scarf & gold earrings, 1990s............................ **400-500**

Rick Wisecarver - Mammy w/a butter churn, standing next to little boy, 1990s.................................... **350-450**

Regal China Cookie Jarrin's Little Angel

Regal China "Cookie Jarrin's Little Angel," black girl w/washboard in washtub, marked & dated "1992" (ILLUS.) .... **400+**

Wisecarver Miss America Cookie Jar

Rockingham Mammy & Clown Cookie Jars

Rick Wisecarver - Miss America, young woman wearing a tiara, in a long pink dress & carrying a bouquet of red roses, 1990s (ILLUS. previous page) **500-600**

Rick Wisecarver - Pappy bust, black man wearing a wide-brimmed hat, 1990s **400-500**

Rick Wisecarver - Saturday night bath, mother & two children, boy & girl in a washtub, 1990s **350-400**

Rockingham Black Clown, dark brown glaze, matches Rockingham Mammy cookie jars, ca. 1960s (ILLUS. right with two Rockingham Mammy jars) **550**

Rockingham Mammy, dark brown glaze, double buttons on the lid forming her stomach, original version, ca. 1960s, rare (ILLUS., top of page above center with other Rockingham cookie jars) **1,000**

Rockingham Mammy, terra cotta brown glossy glaze, lid of the jar is her stomach, Sarsaparilla Decodesign, New York, New York, 1980, made in Japan (ILLUS. above left with other Rockingham cookie jars) **600**

Sears, Roebuck Little Girl Cookie Jar

Sears, Roebuck and Co., little baby girl w/oversized head, curly hair, wearing pink dress & holding a cookie, Japan, 1978 (ILLUS.) **400-600**

Seymour Mann Mammy, McCoy lookalike, black dress, blue top ... **600-800**

Two Seymour Mann Mammy Cookie Jars

Seymour Mann Mammy, McCoy lookalike, different color combination, pink dress, blue top (ILLUS. above right) .... **600+**

Seymour Mann Mammy, McCoy lookalike, lime green dress, pink top (ILLUS. above left) **600-800**

Seymour Mann Mammy, McCoy lookalike, yellow dress, green top **600-800**

"Someone's in the Kitchen" Mammy, figure w/mixing bowl, yellow & white, Dept. 56 .... **350-450**

Star Burst Chef, resembles the National Silver Co. Chef **300-350**

The Bell Captain, head w/wide red-lipped grin, yellow cap, heart-shaped impressed mark "MC/ME © 1992 U.S.A.," 10" h. **350-400**

The Black Ones of California, Big Mama, green dress w/white collar & cuffs, red checked apron & yellow kerchief, contemporary (ILLUS. right)... **450**

Big Mama by Black Ones of California

Two Tri-Star Mammy Cookie Jars

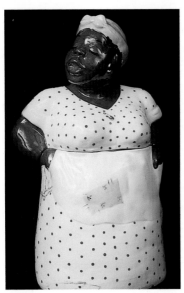

Sister Sookie - Black Ones of California

The Black Ones of California, Sister Sookie, white dress w/small red polka dots & white apron w/blue pocket, blue kerchief, contemporary (ILLUS. left) **450**

Tri-Star Mammy, designed by Linda Kulhanek, unmarked, two versions shown w/patchwork aprons, modern, each (ILLUS. of two above) **400-500**

Weller Mammy, Weller Pottery, 1935, only 144 jars known to exist, 11" h. **2,500+**

White crock-shaped jar, red handle, scene of black woman holding rolling pin in one hand & chastising young boy who was stealing cookies .... **4,000+**

— Chapter 4 —
DOLLS

Rare Folk Art Electric Automaton Scene

Copy of Vintage Automaton

Automaton, Black magician, musical-type, of newer vintage, styled after original French piece by Lambert or Vichy, the black magician standing behind small table & when activated turns his head & lifts the cones in his hands, something different appears under cones each time, 18" h. (ILLUS.) . **$1,495**

Automaton, carved & painted wood, electrical vignette scene, on rectangular base fitted w/long drawer, the painted scenic backdrop gallery on top surrounding scene w/several black characters, some playing music & dancing, also a man feeding chickens, a woman spanking her child as well as Amos 'n' Andy in their taxi & a primitive-looking Mickey Mouse, in the background a rolling linen banner reading "Have You Lost Your Dog?," ca. 1930s, some characters w/cracks & paint flaking, background w/flaking & foxing, 14 x 28", 18" h. (ILLUS. above)....... **4,680**

English 1950s Black Baby Doll

Black baby doll, hard plastic, applied
curly hair, opens & closes eyes,
turns head, by Pedrigree,
England, ca. 1950s (ILLUS.).............. **400**

Palitoy Black Toddler Walking Doll

Black toddler walking doll, hard plastic, applied curly hair, walks, opens &
closes eyes & turns head, by Palitoy,
England, ca. 1950s (ILLUS.)................ **400**

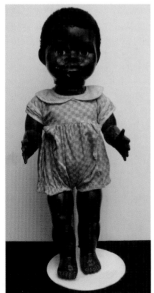

English Black Toddler Walking Doll

Black toddler walking doll, hard
plastic, applied curly hair, eyes
open & close, by Pedrigree,
England, ca. 1950s (ILLUS.)............... **450**

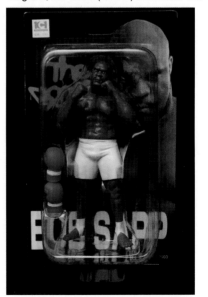

Bob Sapp Wrestling Doll

Bob Sapp doll, based on World
Championship Wrestling star, produced by Hao in China, 2003, near
mint in box (ILLUS.).............................. **50**

Another Bob Sapp Wrestler Doll

Bob Sapp doll, based on World Championship Wrestling star, produced by Hao in China, 2003, near mint in box (ILLUS.) **95**

Booker T. Wrestling Series Doll

Booker T., jointed vinyl, World Championship Wrestling Ring Fighters series by Toy Biz, Inc., 1999, in original package (ILLUS.) **35**

Rare Martha Chase Mammy Doll

Chase (Martha) black Mammy doll, oil-painted stockinette head w/ethnic features, painted eyes, accented nostrils, closed smiling mouth, applied ears, original curly black caracul wig, cloth body w/sateen covering jointed at shoulders, elbows, hips & knees, stitched fingers w/applied thumb, stitched toes, wearing a paisley print dress, probably original, replaced underclothing, wig & features slightly worn, mended tear in sateen on torso, very rare, late 19th - early 20th c., 27" h. (ILLUS.) **5,700**

Cloth doll, cloth, folk art style black boy w/stitched facial features, wearing red outfit w/white shirt, 12 1/2" h. (ILLUS. right), top next page **165**

Cloth doll, cloth, folk art style black girl w/stitched facial features, partially dressed, 12 1/2" h. (ILLUS. left, top next page) **209**

Two Black Folk Art Dolls

General Colin Powell - G.I. Joe Doll

Colin L. Powell doll, part of the "G.I. Joe Classic Collection," wearing his uniform as general, by Hasbro, Inc., 1998, near mint in box (ILLUS.) **300**

De La Soul dolls, jointed vinyl, figures of Pos, Dave & Maseo dressed as astronauts, box marked "De La Soul -

Objective Save Hip Hop," by Maru & Daisy Age, Inc., made in China, 2003, each (ILLUS. of three, top next page)..... **75**

Dennis Rodman Wedding Day Doll

Dennis Rodman doll, "Wedding Day," Rodman dressed in bridal attire, by Street Players, near mint in box (ILLUS.) **125**

"Objective Save Hip Hop" Astronaut Dolls

Destiny's Child Doll Set

Destiny's Child dolls, vinyl, includes Kelly, Beyonce & Michelle, by Hasbro, 2001, each near mint in box, the set of 3 (ILLUS.) **225**

Diahann Carroll "Julia" Doll

Diahann Carroll doll, "Julia," from the T.V. series, Twist n' Turn model, wearing one-piece nurse's outfit, 1968, near mint in box (ILLUS.) **250**

Diana Ross Doll & Original Box

Diana Ross doll, jointed vinyl in famous costume, "Diana Ross of The Supremes" on original box, Ideal, 1969, near mint in original box, 18" h. (ILLUS.)..................................... **500**

Diana Ross Doll in Box by Mego

Diana Ross doll, jointed vinyl in ornate costume, large photo of Ross on box, from Motown Record Corp., made by Mego, 1977, near mint in original box, 12 1/4" h. (ILLUS.) **300**

Family group, homemade carved & painted wood & cloth w/wrapped wire limbs, includes preacher w/white collar, woman wearing blue checked dress & white apron, man wearing dark sweater & white pants, woman wearing long blue lace-trimmed dress & matching hat, boy wearing dark red velvet jacket & pants, girl wearing tan dress w/lace collar & another girl wearing a dark red velvet dress, early, possibly 19th c., the set (ILLUS. of all top of pages 90 & 91) .... **1,000+**

Four of Eight Homemade Black Family Dolls

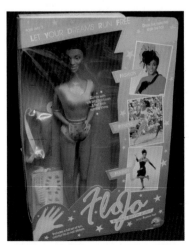

Florence Griffith Joyner "FloJo" Doll

Godfather Wrestling Doll in Package

Four of Eight Homemade Black Family Dolls

Halle Berry "Jinx" Character Doll

Florence Griffith Joyner doll, "Flo-Jo," w/various accessories, by LJN, 1989, near mint in box (ILLUS. bottom left of previous page) **75**

Godfather, jointed vinyl, World Wrestling Federation Road Rage series, by Titan Sports, Inc., 1999, in original package (ILLUS. bottom right of previous page)...................................... **30**

Halle Berry, jointed vinyl, in the character of Jinx from the James Bond movie "Die Another Day," marked "Sideshow Collectibles" (ILLUS. left) **45**

Heinrich Handwerck Black Bisque Girl

Handwerck (Heinrich) black socket head girl, marked "Germany - Heinrich Handwerck - Simon & Halbig - 3 1/2," brown bisque head w/brown sleep eyes, molded & feathered brows, open mouth w/four upper teeth, pierced ears, black mohair wig, jointed wood & composition painted brown body, redressed in new red calico dress, antique underclothing & white pinafore, new cotton socks, old black shoes, 22" (ILLUS.) **1,900**

"Julia" doll clothing set, for "Julia" doll based on TV series, the "Brrr-Furrr" set includes matching coat w/attached belt, fur hat, blue hinge-tongue shoes, booklet, label on box, store sticker, ca. 1969, never removed from box (box discolored w/worn corners) .... **140+**

Jumeau (E). bisque socket-head black girl, marked "Depose - Jumeau - 8" on back of head, lower back stamped "Jumeau - Medaille d'Or - Paris," brown bisque head w/set brown glass eyes, heavy feathered brows, painted upper & lower lashes, closed mouth, pierced applied ears, scrappy original black mohair wig on cork pate, jointed brown composition body w/straight wrists, wearing a pale pink flowered Jumeau-type chemise, antique underclothing, new socks & shoes, head broken & repaired, good finish on body, 18 1/2" (ILLUS.) **1,430**

Tall Jumeau Black Girl Doll

Beloved Belindy Doll in Original Box

Knickerbocker cloth "Beloved Belindy," round paper hang-tag marked "Raggedy Ann's Beloved Belindy - A Character Created by Johnny Gruelle - © Bobbs-Merrill Co., Inc., 1965 - Joy of a Toy™ - Knickerbocker - Knickerbocker Toy Company Inc., New York, U.S.A. - Exclusive Manufacturer," dress tag reads "Beloved Belindy - © Bobbs-Merrill Co., Inc. 1965 - CAL-T-5 All New Material," brown body, black plastic disk eyes w/white circles, single stroke brows, red triangle nose, closed smiling mouth surrounded by white area, jointed at shoulders, elbows, hips & knees, red & white striped legs w/red feet, wearing original red kerchief, dress w/red & white polka dot bodice & yellow & white skirt w/white apron, pantaloons, unplayed-with in original box, 15" (ILLUS.)........................... **925**

Knit Yarn Black Doll

Knit yarn girl, black yarn body & hair w/green hairbow & green dress & neck band, sewn-on red mouth & black & white eyes (ILLUS.).............. **45+**

Special Promotional Kobe Bryant Doll

Kobe Bryant doll, special Adidas promotional piece, complete w/Adidas sneakers & sweatsuit, not widely distributed, near mint in box, 2001 (ILLUS.)... **300**

Kuhnlenz Black Mammy & Baby Dolls

Kuhnlenz (Gebruder) bisque socket head black Mammy & baby, marked "34.17," black head w/set dark pupiless eyes, open mouth w/four upper teeth, yarn or string wig, five-piece composition body w/molded & painted socks & shoes, wearing original red & white dress w/stars, brown plaid shawl & bandanna & white lace-trimmed apron, holding unjointed bisque white baby w/molded bonnet in long lace-trimmed dress, overall excellent condition, 7 1/2" (ILLUS.) **600**

Kuhnlenz (Gebruder) black girl, bisque socket head, marked "34.27," brown sleep eyes, feathered brows, broad nose, open mouth w/four upper teeth, black human hair wig, jointed wood & composition body w/jointed wrists, wearing a pink dress w/lace trim, new underclothing, socks & shoes, tiny chip on upper lid at outside corner of right eye, late French-type body 6 w/left second finger replaced, Germany, early 20th c., 17" h. **2,100**

Marla Gibbs T.V. Character Doll

Marla Gibbs doll, based on her character from the T.V. show "The Jeffersons," by Shindana Toys, Inc., 1978, near mint in box, 15 1/2" h. (ILLUS.) **200**

MC Hammer "U Can't Touch This" Doll

MC Hammer doll, dressed in fancy performance costume, includes a cassette tape of "U Can't Touch This," by Mattel, 1991, near mint in box (ILLUS.) **50**

MC Hammer Doll with Boom Box

MC Hammer doll, dressed in fancy performance costume, includes boom box playing rap music, by Mattel, 1991, near mint in box (ILLUS.)....... **50**

Battery-operated Michael Jackson Doll

Michael Jackson doll, battery-operated, plays "Black/White," by Street Life, 1991, near mint in box (ILLUS. previous page) **125**

Michael Jackson "Beat It" Doll

Michael Jackson doll, "Beat It," based on his record album, by MJJ Productions, 1984 (ILLUS.) **75**

Michael Jackson Grammy Awards Doll

Michael Jackson doll, "Grammy Awards," wearing the outfit he wore to the awards program, by MJJ Productions, 1984 (ILLUS.)....................... **75**

Michael Todd Duncan "Balthazar" Doll

Michael Todd Duncan doll, jointed vinyl, in the character of Balthazar from movie "The Scorpion King," produced by Jakks Pacific, Inc. 2002 (ILLUS. in original package)........ **55**

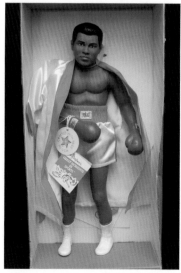

Scarce Muhammad Ali Effanbee Doll

Muhammad Ali doll, vinyl, jointed, wearing boxing outfit, Effanbee Doll Corp., 1986, near mint in box, 18" h. (ILLUS.) **450**

Pair of Black Ragtime Kids Dolls

Papier-mâché "Ragtime Kids," marked on round attached tags "Ragtime Kids - Name Registered - 'Alexander' - 'Bavaria,' & 'R.O.L.' - Trade Mark," papier-mâché brown heads w/exaggerated ethnic features, painted brown eyes, closed mouth, molded & black-painted curly hair, cloth bodies w/composition hands, girl w/black felt legs, boy w/pink cloth legs & long thin oilcloth feet, in original clothing, boy wearing white two-piece suit w/white shirt & black tie, matching white hat w/black ribbon band, girl wearing white dress w/pink ribbon trim & pompons, net collar & stiff crinoline underclothing, unplayed-with, early 20th c., 12 1/2" & 13", pr. (ILLUS.)...... **950**

Rag doll, black cloth head in one piece w/torso, embroidered white triangles w/black shoebuttons for eyes, brown embroidered brows, red embroidered mouth w/five white embroidered teeth, hair of black rags tied in knot & stitched in circles around the back, cloth body w/arms & legs made separately & stitched onto torso, stitched fingers & sepa-

Large Primitive Rag Doll with Smile

rate thumb, wearing probably original blue & white flowered dress w/black & white flowered sleeves, underclothing, black lace-up baby shoes, apparently all hand-stitched, only minor wear & repairs, late 19th - early 20th c., 27" (ILLUS.)............ **1,125**

Large Primitive Black Rag Doll

Rag doll, black cloth head in one piece w/torso, eyes, brows & mouth stitched w/heavy thread, applied nose & ears, hair indicated by ribbed fabric sewn to back of head, cloth body w/arms & legs sewn separately & attached, stitched fingers & separate thumb, legs w/center seams on front & back but no toes, stuffed w/cotton, fabric legs pieced together, wearing faded gold dress w/mended places that could be original, some fading, late 19th - early 20th c., 22" (ILLUS. previous page)... **575**

Black Smiling Lady Rag Doll

Rag doll, black cloth head w/black button eyes w/embroidered whites, needle sculptured nose, embroidered open-closed smiling mouth w/two teeth, needle sculptured ears w/earrings, black string & braided fabric hair, cloth black body jointed at shoulders, stitched fingers & toes, excelsior-stuffed, wearing probably original white blouse, print skirt, tan apron, slip, no socks or shoes, overall excellent condition, late 19th - early 20th c., 16" (ILLUS.).................... **375**

Rag doll, black cloth head w/embroidered facial features, needle-sculptured nose, applied ears, short curly wool hair, cloth brown body w/arms

Black Rag Doll with Original Clothing & legs sewn on, stitched fingers but no thumb, wearing original blue print dress, white apron & neckerchief, original plain muslin underclothing w/no lace, white cotton socks w/red ribbon garters, black home-made leather shoes, plaid bandanna, glass bead necklace & loop earrings, excellent condition, late 19th - early 20th c., 13" (ILLUS.)............................ **600**

Sad-looking Black Rag Cloth Doll

Rag doll, black cloth head w/small white button eyes, black caracul eyebrows, needle-sculptured nose w/embroidered nostrils, embroidered downturned mouth w/space between lips, black caracul wig, black cloth body jointed at shoulders, mitten hands, wearing possibly original white cotton dress w/brown print & trimmed w/ruffles made of white cotton w/small red polka dots, underclothing, black stockings & leather high-button boots, some wear, fading & mended holes, late 19th - early 20th c., 25" (ILLUS. previous page) **325**

floss embroidery, body stitch-jointed at shoulders, elbows, hips & knees, no detail of fingers or toes on hands & feet, wearing plaid dress w/smocked bodice, large white collar & cuffs, matching pants, white apron w/eyelet trim, light wear, spots of soil on upper left leg, early 20th c., 22" (ILLUS.) **400**

Large Black Stuffed Rag Doll

Rag doll, black-dyed softly stuffed muslin body w/unjointed neck, glass eyes, fur brows, applied nose, mouth & ears, black hair attached w/skin strips, no fingers or toes, wearing very plain probably original brown print dress, white slip & pants, black wool socks, 27" (ILLUS.) **1,000**

Black Rag Doll with Embroidery

Rag doll, black cloth w/unjointed neck, facial features embroidered w/tan floss, hair indicated w/black

Doll Series with Run, Jam & Master Jay

RUN-DMC dolls, jointed vinyl, figures of singers Run, Jam & Master Jay, the RUN-DMC series, produced by Mezco Toys 2002, all in red outfits, in original packages, set of three (ILLUS. bottom previous page) **200**

Snoop Dogg Doll & Box

Snoop Dogg doll, vinyl, fully articulated, wearing Adidas shoes, gold chains & braided hair, by Vital Toys LLC., w/original box (ILLUS.) **35**

Rare Steiff Black Girl Doll

Steiff black girl doll, black pressed felt face w/center seem, black shoe button eyes w/white felt behind, accented nostrils, red felt mouth w/white line between lips, applied ears, black mohair wig, black felt body jointed at shoulders & hips, stitched fingers & toes on oversized feet, wearing a black & white striped silk dress, panties, large bow in hair, excellent condition, dress splitting, Steiff button w/underlined "ff" in left ear, early 20th c., 19" h. (ILLUS.).... **2,200**

Finely Detailed Black Stockinette Doll

Stockinette black lady, black stockinette head sewn on black cloth body, exaggerated needle sculptured features, black shoe button eyes w/white backgrounds, black embroidered brows, red embroidered nostril accents, red embroidered mouth, needle sculptured ears, short black wool curls, cloth body w/upper arms, lower arms, upper legs & lower legs made separately & sewn together, mitten hands w/stitched thumb, front of foot made separately, bias tape down back seam, wearing probably original red print dress, white apron & pants, overall excellent condition, late 19th - early 20th c., 20" (ILLUS.) **1,025**

Stockinette black lady, handmade
w/stockinette head w/needle-sculpt-
ed nose, ears & chin, painted eyes
& mouth, wire earrings, yarn braids
attached to head, black cloth body
w/no indication of fingers on hands,
feet shaped w/light wire & stitched,
wearing original red & white polka
dot dress w/black shoe buttons on
front, white apron, original underclothing, painted brown shoes,
completely hand-stitched, unmarked, 16" (three yarn braids may
have been added at a different time
as the yarn is heavier) **425**

Stuffed Cloth Native Girl Doll

Stuffed cloth native girl, brown sewn
fabric body & head w/red blouse &
brown beaded skirts, beaded jewel-
ry & ornate tall head band, sewn-on
facial features (ILLUS.)..................... **100+**

Scarce WPA Little Black Sambo Doll

**Stockinette WPA Little Black Sam-
bo,** stamped on lower back "WPA -
Handicraft - Project #860 - Milwaukee, Wisconsin - Sponsored by Milwaukee County and Milwaukee
State Teachers College," also
marked on jacket & shoes "Designed by Helen Clark," the stockinette head painted brown w/brown
eyes, closed mouth, curly black cotton string hair, brown cloth body
tab-jointed at shoulders & hips,
stitched fingers & separate thumb,
hard soles on round feet w/no toes,
wearing original red double-breast-
ed jacket, blue short pants & purple
& red shoes, slight fading & wear,
1930s, 22" (ILLUS.) **1,850**

Terri Lee "Patti Jo" Girl Doll

Terri Lee "Patti Jo," marked "Terri
Lee" on head, "Terri Lee - Pat.
Pending" on back, Terri Lee tag on
the coat, brown hard plastic head,
painted brown eyes, accented nostrils, closed red mouth, original
black synthetic wig, five-piece hard

plastic body, wearing blue & white gingham dress w/white pleated trim, matching panties, replaced socks & vinyl shoes, navy blue coat w/red trim, black snood on hair, some flaking on body & slight color wear, 1950s, 16" (ILLUS. previous page)..... **525**

Scarce Tony Sarg "Mammy Doll"

Tony Sarg's "Mammy Doll," composition, w/original red & white kerchief & dress & white apron, w/original hangtag, holding matching white composition baby, w/original box, ca. 1930s, Mammy doll 17" h. (ILLUS.)..... **1,100-1,200**

Discontinued Tupac Shakur Doll

Tupac Shakur doll, jointed vinyl, from All Entertainment, Inc., China, 2002, produced without proper permission & discontinued (ILLUS.)........ **250**

Venus & Serena Doll Set

Venus & Serena dolls, part of "American Champions" series, each fully articulated, w/tennis racquets, tennis ball, jackets & water bottles, by Play Along, Inc., Florida, 2000, near mint in box (ILLUS.) **75**

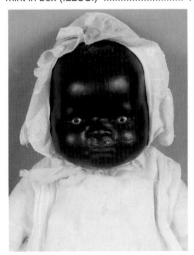

Black Wax Bye-Lo Baby

Wax Bye-Lo Baby, no legible marks, black wax flange head, set brown eyes, closed mouth, roughness on top of head indicating hair, white muslin body, black poured wax hands, "frog" legs, working crier, wearing a white baby dress & slip made w/old fabric, diaper, romper, new booties & bonnet, some wear to lip color, 15" (ILLUS.) **220**

Black Wax Dream Baby Doll

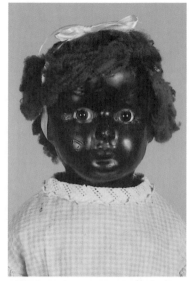

Wax Over Composition Black Girl Doll

Wax Dream Baby, marked "A.M. - 341 - Germany," poured black wax head, set brown glass eyes, closed mouth, cloth body w/black wax over composition hands, wearing a white baby dress made w/early fabric, old slip & flannel diaper, antique bonnet, only light flaking, shoulder seams restitched, 17" (ILLUS.) **468**

Wax shoulder-head black girl, the head in wax over composition, set brown eyes, closed mouth, original fuzzy black hair, white cloth excelsior-stuffed body w/black wax over composition lower arms, black cloth lower legs, wearing antique half-slip, new black cotton socks, antique lace-up shoes, wax aged w/a few cracks, wear on lip color, lower legs possibly replaced, 23" h. (ILLUS. top right) **275**

Wilma doll, jointed vinyl, represents the young black girl integrating a school, based on a Norman Rockwell illustration, Rumble Seat Press, Germany, 1964, near mint in box, 9" h. (ILLUS. right) **250**

Wilma Doll Based on Rockwell Scene

Will Smith - Agent Jay Action Doll

Will Smith action figure, dressed as Agent Jay from the movie "Men in Black II," Columbia Pictures, Hasbro, 2002, near mint in original box (ILLUS.) **55**

Will Smith - James West Action Doll

Will Smith action figure, dressed as James West from the movie "Wild, Wild West," Warner Brothers, WB Toys, 1999, near mint in original box (ILLUS.) **65**

— Chapter 5 —
FIGURAL & MISCELLANEOUS ITEMS

Rare Animated Alarm Clock

Alarm clock, windup metal animated-type, round case on slender legs & bell on top, paper lithographed face w/color scene of black woman rocking black child in cradle, foot & cradle are supposed to move, not working, probably German, early 20th c., 6" h. (ILLUS.) **$605**

Andirons, cast iron, figural, cast as black man & black woman dressed in early 19th c. attire, found in Georgia, overall deep pitting, first half 19th c., 16 1/2" h., pr......................... **825**

Cast-iron African-American Pieces

Andirons, cast iron, figure of African-American man standing w/hands on bent knees, early paint w/white shirt, red pants, black skin & painted facial features, ca. 1870, paint imperfections, minor corrosion, 12 1/2 x 16 1/2", 19 1/2" h., pr. (ILLUS. left & right with hitching post finial) **1,380**

Figural Chalkware Bank

Bank, chalkware, figure of a black man seated playing a large drum, marked "L - M," ca. 1950s (ILLUS.).... **150**

Rare Figural Majolica Black Girl Bell

Bell, majolica, figural, a standing black child w/one hand to her face, wearing long pink dress, white apron & blue cap, late 19th - early 20th c., 8 1/4" h. (ILLUS.)............................. **1,150**

Three Liquor Decantors are made by Baccarat

Bottle, figural, for liquor, Negro Lady, clear frosted mold-blown body w/black glass head w/red lips forming stopper, ca. 1880-1920, probably French, 12 1/4" h. (ILLUS. above center with waiter bottles) **450-750**

Bottle, figural, for liquor, Negro Waiter, clear unfrosted body w/black glass head w/red lips forming stopper, ca. 1880-1920, possibly French, 12 1/4" h. (ILLUS. left with other waiter & lady bottle) **450-750**

Bottle, figural, for liquor, Negro Waiter, frosted clear body w/black glass head w/red lips forming stopper, ca. 1880-1920, possibly French, 12 1/4" h. (ILLUS. right with other waiter & lady bottle) **450-750**

Bottle opener, "Alligator with boy," cast-iron figural, a black boy wearing a white shirt & pants being bitten in the behind by an alligator, difficult to find, reference No. F-133, NOTE: this opener has been reproduced; the copies have a red line around the alligator's eye not seen in the original; 3" h. (ILLUS. left with other boy & alligator, below) **75-150**

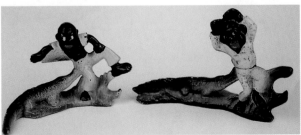

Two Alligator with Black Boy Bottle Openers

Bottle opener, "Alligator with boy with hands up," cast-iron figural, a black boy wearing a white shirt & pants being bitten in the behind by an alligator, difficult to find, reference No. F-134, 2 3/4" h. (ILLUS. right with other alligator & boy opener on previous page) **75-150**

Black Face Wall-mount Bottle Opener

Bottle opener, "Black face," wall-mounted, cast-iron, black man's face w/large red mouth & hole in the ears, marked "Crowley," reference No. F-404, 4" h. (ILLUS.) **350-550**

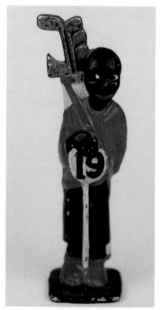

Scarce Black Caddy Bottle Opener

Bottle opener, "Caddy," cast-iron figural, a black boy wearing a red shirt, black pants & red shoes, holding a

golf bag w/clubs & resting his hand on a white sign that reads "19," very hard to find, reference No. F-44, 5 7/8" h. (ILLUS.) **250-350**

Wall-mounted Four-eye Black Lady Bottle Opener

Bottle opener, "Florida Pipe & Foundry," wall-mounted, cast-iron, four-eyed black woman w/red hair & lips, wearing bonnet that reads "Florida Pipe & Foundry," rare, reference No. F-410, 4 1/8" h. (ILLUS.) .... **550+**

Grass Skirt Greek Bottle Opener

Bottle opener, "Grass Skirt Greek," cast-iron figural, a black boy wearing a grass skirt, clutching a sign that reads "Phi Gamma Delta - Fiji Island Party - '53," very hard to find, reference No. F-43, 5" h. (ILLUS.) **250-350**

Black Man on Cotton Bale Figural Box

Box, cov., ceramic, figural, well-dressed black man wearing white top hat & suit seated on bale of cotton that forms the box base, cream-colored w/touches of tan, dark brown & black, ca. 1980s (ILLUS.) **200**

Slave Branding Iron

Branding iron, antebellum slave branding iron bearing initials "E.F." (ILLUS.) **1,100**

Bust of a black man, carved & painted wood, mounted on black-painted plinth, 19th c., 3" w., 8 1/8" h. (wear) **1,265**

Bust of a black man, ceramic, holding pineapple in his arms, black w/gold hair & pineapple, by WOR, 1950s, Collection of Roger Chin (ILLUS. top next column).. **150**

1950s Bust of a Black Man & Pineapple

Bust of a blackamoor, composition or plaster-of-Paris, the head topped by large beribboned turban, wearing large earrings & banded collar w/star-form pin, raised on round black base, decorated in shades of tan, brown, gold & black, ca. 1950, large **75-125**

Fine Terra Cotta Bust of a Blackamoor

Bust of a blackamoor, hand-painted terra cotta, bearded black man dressed as Arab, raised on squared, stepped pedestal base, Austria, Collection of John Walker Antiques and Objets de Vertu (ILLUS.)................... **3,000**

Bust of a blackamoor, hand-painted terra cotta, young black man wearing turban, large bead necklace & striped wrap, signed in back, ca. 1842, Collection of John Walker Antiques and Objets de Vertu **4,400**

Majolica Black Banjo Player Figure

Bust figure, majolica, half-length figure of black banjo player, marked "3407," late 19th - early 20th c., 8" h. (ILLUS.) **850**

Bourbon Street Serenade Bust Figure

Bust statue, ceramic, "All That Jazz - Bourbon Street Serenade," portrait of New Orleans black musician playing clarinet, limited edition of 950, produced by Willitts Galleries 2003, 20 1/2" h. (ILLUS.) **1,200**

All Night Long Musician Bust Figure

Bust statue, ceramic, "All That Jazz - All Night Long," portrait of black musician playing saxophone, limited edition of 1,250, produced by Willitts Galleries 2003, 32" h. (ILLUS.) ... **750**

Bust Figure of Salome

Bust statue, ceramic, biblical character Salome, wearing exotic headdress & low-cut gown, ca. 1940, 27" h. (ILLUS.)................................. **1,200**

Josephine Baker-style Bust Figure

Bust statue, ceramic, black woman w/bunch of bananas, inspired by entertainer Josephine Baker, marked "CIADA," ca. 1940s (ILLUS.) **650**

Candy holder, figural papier-mâché, grotesque caricature of standing black boy wearing blue jacket, white shirt, red bow tie & pants, exaggerated lips & bare feet, opening in top of head, bright colors, ca. 1900, 3 1/2" w., 5 1/2" h. (ILLUS. top right column **130**

Black Boy Figural Candy Holder

Cane, carved antler handle, carved in the form of a frightened black man w/carved inset head, his upper torso surrounded by rolled ring, his lower body being attacked by an alligator, Collection of John Walker Antiques & Objets de Vertu (ILLUS. above) **1,500**

Cane, carved antler handle, carved in the form of a seated black man w/carved inset head, holding onto tail of alligator, silver metal ferrule & wooden shaft, Collection of John Walker Antiques & Objets de Vertu (ILLUS., below)................................ **1,500**

Carved Cane with Frightened Man

Man & Alligator Carved Cane Handle

Fine Cane Carved with a Man's Head

Cane, the carved wooden handle in the form of a realistic smiling bearded black man, silver ferrule & dark wood shaft, head w/inset teeth & glass eyes, Collection of John Walker Antiques & Objets de Vertu (ILLUS.)........ **875**

Canvas sack, printed in black, red & green, titled "A Watermelon Frolic," large central caricature of black man surrounded by wedges of watermelon, copyright by I.M. Yunger, printed by E.I.H., New York, 1900 (ILLUS. top right) **600-800**

Clock, bronzed cast-metal, figural, the cast in the form of a large shaggy walking dog w/African-American newsboy on his back, the dial of clock in the side of the dog, dial marked "Regent Mfg. Co., Chicago," works stamped "Patented...Jan. 13, 1891," not working, 7" l. (ILLUS. right) **288**

Unusual Early Printed Canvas Sack

Dog & Black Newsboy Clock

Cast-iron Figural Blackamoor Clock

Clock, cast iron, figural, standing bearded blackamoor w/feather headdress, earrings & beaded necklaces, the clock dial w/Roman numerals in his stomach, standing on round, stepped base, France, ca. 1900, Collection of John Walker Antiques & Objets de Vertu (ILLUS.) **1,800**

Clock with Figural Black Children

Clock, table model, brass & cast metal, a tall openwork framework w/figures of seven black children, a brass clock face suspended at the top center, Austria, ca. 1900, very rare (ILLUS.) **3,500**

Figural Cast-metal Mammy Wall Clock

Clock, wall-type, cast-metal figure of black Mammy standing w/hands on hips, clock dial forming the front of her dress, worn paint, Admiral Mfg. Co., ca. 1910 (ILLUS.) **1,200**

Clock, wall-type, figural black elf, Miken, Japan (ILLUS. bottom left with other wall clocks, top next page) **200**

Clock, wall-type, flat cut-out of black boy w/red polka dot tie, blue jacket, yellow pants & red cap & shoes, playing accordion, Germany, 20th c. (ILLUS. next page top center with other wall clocks) **250**

Clock, wall-type, head of black man wearing green derby hat & red tie pendulum, Lux Clock Co., Waterbury, Connecticut, first half 20th c. (ILLUS. next page right with other wall clocks) **350**

Group of Figural Wall Clocks

Unusual Enamel-decorated Decanter

Decanter w/original stopper, sapphire blue footed tapering cylindrical body w/narrow shoulder & tall slender neck w/flared rim, finely enameled w/scene of dancing black minstrel wearing striped pants, long-tailed jacket & carrying a cane & top hat, enameled title "Cake Walk" under the figure, clear facet-cut mushroom stopper, Europe, late 19th c., 11 1/4" h. (ILLUS.) **200-250**

Doorstop, cast iron, figural black man carrying satchel & looking back over his shoulder, Hubley, 5 1/8" w., 7 1/2" h. **950**

Figure group, porcelain, young black girl refusing to share her fan w/her younger brother, titled "Don't even think of it," based on early illustration, made in Italy, modern (ILLUS. next page) **250**

Figure Group of Two Black Children

Figure group, Staffordshire pottery, "Topsy and Eva," standing young white girl w/brown hair holding book in one hand & small black child in other arm, ca. 1860, some wear, 5 1/4" h. (ILLUS. right with Jim Crow figure, bottom of page 117) **259**

Figure group, Staffordshire pottery, "Uncle Tom and Eva," black man seated on bale of cotton w/young girl standing on bale beside him, worn polychrome decoration, ca. 1860, 6" l., 11" h. (ILLUS. next column) **288**

Large Uncle Tom & Eva Pottery Group

Figure group, Staffordshire pottery, "Uncle Tom and Eva," black man wearing striped pants standing in orange row boat, one arm leaning on upright oar, the other arm around small white girl standing on bale of cotton, molded blue waves below the boat, molded title on oval base, small glaze flake on edge of boat, ca. 1860, 12" h. (ILLUS. center with two other Uncle Tom & Eva groups, below).................................. **1,100**

Three Varied Uncle Tom & Eva Staffordshire Groups

Figure group, Staffordshire pottery, "Uncle Tom and Eva," seated black man holding book w/one hand, his other arm around young white girl w/long brown hair seated on his knee, his straw hat at his side, oval base w/molded title, polychrome decoration, ca. 1860, flake on nose of child, 8 1/2" h. (ILLUS. left with Uncle Tom & Eva in boat & larger seated grouping, previous page) **303**

Fine Uncle Tom and Eva Figure Group

Figure group, Staffordshire pottery, "Uncle Tom and Eva," seated black man holding book in one arm, his other arm around young white girl w/long brown hair wearing full skirt & holding large yellow hat, polychrome decoration, ca. 1860, minor paint wear, 8 1/2" h. (ILLUS.) **345**

Figure group, Staffordshire pottery, "Uncle Tom and Eva," seated black man holding his yellow hat in one hand, his other arm around young white girl w/long brown hair standing on his knee, oval base w/molded title, polychrome decoration, ca. 1860, chip on edge of hat, some glaze & paint loss, ca. 1860, 11" h. (ILLUS. right with Uncle Tom & Eva in boat & other group, previous page).................. **468**

Figure of a black boy, bisque, seated on chamber pot eating slice of watermelon, Germany, late 19th - early 20th c. **145**

Figure of a black boy, terra cotta, standing wearing hand-painted yellow robe w/ruffled collar, by Goldscheider, Collection of John Walker Antiques & Objets de Vertu **1,250**

Goldscheider Black Clown Figure

Figure of a black clown, terra cotta, standing wearing a long cape w/ruffled collar, one arm bent up & pointing, marked "Goldscheider 1089," Austria, early 20th c., 14 1/4" h. (ILLUS.) **1,500**

Figure of a black man, bisque, standing & holding a chicken, fine coloring, late 19th c., 7 1/2" h..................... **250**

Figure of a blackamoor lady, bisque, finely hand-painted, standing wearing feathered turban, pale blue skirt w/red & gold belt & pale pink shawl, holding parrot on her raised arm & cornucopia of flowers in other hand, standing in front of green tree stump & raised on round white base w/gold & scroll trim, France, late 19th c., 11" h. (ILLUS. next page) **500-600**

Tall Bisque Figure of Blackamoor Lady

Large Terra Cotta Blackamoor Figures

1950s Figure of African Native

Figure of a kneeling nude, ceramic, stylized figure of African native on oval base, gold neck band, by Alexander Backer, 1950s, Collection of Roger Chin (ILLUS.) **125**

Figures, polychromed terra cotta, full-figure statues of standing blackamoors, each raised on a columnar pedestal w/square base, each w/one arm across chest, one wearing yellow vest & striped orange & white turban, the other an orange-trimmed green vest & blue & white striped turban, Europe, early 20th c., each 52 1/2" h., pr. (ILLUS. top next column) **4,600**

Figures of Blackamoor Musicians

Figures of blackamoor musicians, hand-painted terra cotta, both standing, the woman wearing wide hat, fringed dress & playing cymbals, the man wearing cap, jacket, knee breeches w/a sash & playing a mandolin, each on a green rockwork base, Austria, late 19th c., tall, Collection of John Walker Antiques & Objets de Vertu, pr. (ILLUS. of both).. **3,400**

Black Clown Looking Through Legs

Figurine, ceramic, nodder-type, black clown bent down looking between legs, Japan, ca. 1970s (ILLUS.) **300**

Black Clown with Hands Out Nodder

Figurine, ceramic, nodder-type, black clown holding hands out to sides, Japan, ca. 1970s (ILLUS.)................. **300**

Clown & Umbrella Nodder Figurine

Figurine, ceramic, nodder-type, black clown holding umbrella, both head & feet nod, Japan, ca. 1970s (ILLUS.)... **450**

Black Clown with Bloomers Figurine

Figurine, ceramic, nodder-type, black clown holding bloomers in her hand, Japan, ca. 1970s (ILLUS.)................. **325**

Brayton Petunia & Sambo Figures

Figurine, ceramic, "Petunia," little black girl standing holding a basket & wearing a blue dress & white apron, part of Children's Series by Brayton-Laguna of California, copies are known marked "Occupied Japan," 6 1/4" h. (ILLUS. right with Sambo figurine) **235**

Figurine, ceramic, "Sambo," black boy standing w/a chicken under one arm & wearing blue overalls & a straw hat, part of Children's Series by Brayton-Laguna of California, 7 1/2" h. (ILLUS. left with Petunia figurine) **260**

Figurine, majolica, standing black boy wearing large hat, white shirt & blue pants beside large pale blue cotton basket, on raised oval base, Europe, late 19th c., minor hat chips, several base chips, 9" h. (ILLUS.)...... **495**

Lladro Figurine of Martin Luther King

Figurine, porcelain, Dr. Martin Luther King, Jr., limited edition, Lladro, Spain, 1990 (ILLUS.)......................... **800**

Black Boy & Cotton Basket Figurine

Jim Crow & Topsy & Eva Figures

Blackamoor Man & Woman Figures

Figurine, Staffordshire pottery, "Jim Crow," standing figure of black minstrel man wearing blue striped pants & red vest, playing concertina, on round green base, some wear to paint, ca. 1860, 5 1/4" h. (ILLUS. previous page left with Topsy & Eva group) **345**

Figurines, bisque, finely painted male & female African dancers, each in animated pose w/flowing clothes, she playing a tambourine, he holding cymbals, France, late 19th c., restorations, 26 1/4" h., pr..... **2,500-2,600**

Black Jockey Hitching Post

Figurines, ceramic, Blackamoor Man & Blackamoor Woman, kneeling, 8 1/2" h., pr. (ILLUS. above).......... **80-100**

Hitching post, cast iron, figural standing black jockey on square pedestal base, colorful old repaint, some rust, late 19th - early 20th c., 38" h. (ILLUS. bottom left) **500-1,0000**

Early Black Jockey Hitching Post

Hitching post, cast iron, figure of a black jockey standing & reaching forward w/one arm, other hand in pocket, wearing removable hat, orange vest & brown pants, attached to a square cement block base, good patina, late 19th - early 20th c., 35" h. (ILLUS.)..... **1,265**

Hitching post finial, cast iron, stylized head of African-American man holding a ring & chain in his mouth, 19th c., w/later stand, 5 1/2 x 6", 9 1/2" h. (ILLUS. center with figural andirons, page 104) **2,300**

Figural Foot Incense Burner

Incense burner, ceramic, figural, black boy's head peeking over large feet, smiling face, opening in the back, early 20th c. (ILLUS.) **200**

Inkwell, brass, figural, footed wide dished stand centered by well-modeled head of bearded blackamoor wearing cap & large ring earrings, the hinged cap opening to the inkwell, Collection of John Walker Antiques & Objets de Vertu (ILLUS. of two views, below) **950**

Inkwell, cast bronze, an oblong tray cast at one end w/full-relief head of black boy wearing hat, hinged to show original porcelain well, the lower portion of the tray showing his shirt & a leafy branch, numbered on bottom "4507," late 19th - early 20th c., 3 x 6", 2 1/2" h. (ILLUS. below) **253**

Figural Black Boy Inkwell

Liquor bottles, ceramic, figural blackamoors, colorful painted trim, Italy, ca. 1950s, 6" h., pr. (ILLUS., top next page) **150**

Liquor decanter, ceramic, figural, African woman kneeling holding basket, Drioli Liquor, one of a set of four, Italy, ca. 1960s (ILLUS. next page, lower left) **150**

Two Views of a Figural Brass Inkwell

Figural Italian Liquor Bottles

African Woman with Basket Decanter

Liquor decanter, ceramic, figural, black African man seated playing drum, Drioli Liquor, part of a set of four, Italy, ca. 1960s (ILLUS. right) **150**

African Man Drummer Decanter

Black Minstrel Musician Decanter

Liquor decanter, ceramic, figural, black minstrel man seated on low column, colorfully dressed & holding guitar, Drioli Liquor, part of a set of four, Italy, ca. 1960s (ILLUS.) **150**

Decanter Honoring the Slave "York"

Liquor decanter, ceramic, figural, full-figure of "York," Clark's black slave who accompanied him on the Lewis & Clark Expedition in 1804, marked "Gary Schildt Kentucky Straight Bourbon Whiskey," produced by Alpha Industries, Inc., 1972 (ILLUS.).... **150**

Beam Decanter of John Henry

Liquor decanter, ceramic, figural, "John Henry - A Steel Drivin' Man - Big Bend Tunnel - West Virginia," figure of legendary black railroad track layer, bourbon whiskey, James B. Beam Distilling Co., 1972 (ILLUS.) **150**

Liquor decanter, ceramic, figural, " Kings African Rifle Corps - 1914," standing soldier in uniform commemorating West African British Colonial Army Rifle Unit that fought in World War I, contains cream sherry, bottled by Grenadier Spirits, San Francisco, 1971 (ILLUS. top of next page) **125**

Liquor decanter, ceramic, figural, kneeling figure of African woman dancer leaning backward, part of a four piece set, Drioli Liquor, Italy, ca. 1960s (ILLUS. bottom left of next page) **150**

Antigua Man Figural Decanter

Liquor decanter, ceramic, figural, model of West Indies man seated on barrel & smoking cigarette, barrel inscribed "Antigua B.W.I.," souvenir of island of Antigua in British West Indies, ca. 1950s (ILLUS.) **125**

Kings African Rifle Corps Decanter

African Native Woman Dancer Decanter

Limbo Drummer Rum Decanter

Liquor decanter, ceramic, figural, seated feature of West Indian limbo dance drummer, wearing colorful outfit, a yellow plastic hat forming the stopper, label on front reads "Old Oak Rum - Angostura Bitters - Trinidad, West Indies," ca. 1980s (ILLUS. previous page) **40**

George Washington Carver Decanter

African Woman Liquor Decanter

Liquor decanter, ceramic, figural, stylized model of the head of an African woman wearing many neck rings, metal earrings, molded braided hair & red lip color, cork stopper in top of head, ca. 1950s (ILLUS.) **85**

Liquor decanter, porcelain, figural, "George Washington Carver," noted black scientist, from "The Great Americans" series, bourbon whiskey, McCormick Distilling Co., Weston, Missouri (ILLUS. top right) ... **250**

Liquor decanter, porcelain, figural, "Louis Armstrong," a music box in the base plays "Hello Dolly," bourbon whiskey, McCormick Distilling Co., Weston, Missouri (ILLUS. bottom right) **200**

Louis Armstrong Whiskey Decanter

Lionstone "The Blacksmith" Decanter

Liquor decanter, porcelain, figural, "The Blacksmith," black man standing next to anvil, bourbon whiskey, Lionstone Distilleries, Ltd., Kentucky, 1973 (ILLUS.) **150**

Muhammad Ali Figural Decanter

Liquor decanter, porcelain, figural, "The Greatest," portrait of Muhammad Ali posed in boxing outfit, contains grenadine, McCormick Distilling Co., Weston, Missouri, 1981 (ILLUS.) ... **150**

Two German Black Waiter Decanters

Liquor decanters, majolica, figural, standing black waiter holding tray fitted w/shot glass, one in pink & one in green, Germany, ca. 1940s, each (ILLUS. of two).......................... **450**

Mannequin, life-sized, chalkware & wood, black man wearing black derby hat, dark blue & green checked shirt & dark blue pants, jointed at shoulders, elbows, wrists, neck & mid-body, jointed forefingers & thumb, forehead scarred in decorative fashion w/numerous bumps, late 19th - early 20th c., 19" w. at shoulders, 5' 9" h. (one finger missing, another partially missing)............. **660**

Match box, cov., porcelain, figural, modeled as hand-painted head of blackamoor boy looking upward w/mouth open, his striped turban forming the cover, Germany, ca. 1900, Collection of John Walker Antiques & Objets de Vertu .... **125+**

Medal, anti-slavery, silver (?), central scene of kneeling slave in chains below inscription "Am I Not A Man and a Brother," below the figure in small letters "A Voice From Great Britain to America - 1834," slight wear, hole drilled in top rim, 1 3/4" d.............. **400-450**

Mug, china, transfer-printed color scene of black man playing banjo, Warwick China IOGA mark, early 20th c. **150-200**

Tall Rookwood Mug with Black Boy

Mug, pottery, tall tapering cylindrical shape w/angled handle, painted w/a portrait bust of a scowling young black boy wearing a hat & white shirt, Gorham silver-overlay band at rim & top of handle, Rookwood pottery, Standard glaze, decorated by Grace Young, 1900, 6" d., 7 3/4" h. (ILLUS.) **2,990**

Needlework picture, titled "10 Little Niggers," hand-made w/a row of black boys & girls sewn in yarn on canvas, first half 20th c., framed (ILLUS. below) **250**

Rookwood Mug with Smiling Black Boy

Mug, pottery, baluster shape w/loop handle, painted w/a portrait bust of a smiling young black boy wearing a hat & white shirt, Rookwood pottery, Standard glaze, decorated by Sturgis Laurence, 1896, firing crack in body, 5" d., 5" h. (ILLUS.) **1,610**

Needlework Picture of Black Children

Painting of Black Woman by Walker

metal base, marked "Florenza," 1950s (ILLUS. top of next page) **150**

Walker Painting of "Old Cotton Picker"

Watercolor on Cloth of Black Girl

Painting, oil on academy board, "The Cotton Picker" by William Aiken Walker (American, 1838-1921), scene of older black woman wearing ragged clothes, standing behind large basket of cotton in cotton field, framed, 6 x 12" (ILLUS.) **7,475**

Painting, oil on academy board, "The Old Cotton Picker" by William Aiken Walker (American, 1838-1921), scene of elderly black man wearing ragged clothes & standing in cotton field, framed, 6 x 12" (ILLUS. top right)... **7,180**

Painting, watercolor on fabric, young black girl standing eating a large slice of watermelon, inscribed "Wish you wuz me?" & signed "L.S.", ca. 1920s (ILLUS. bottom right)............. **1,008**

Pencil, mechanical, gilt-metal & beads, the top w/figural blackamoor head wearing gilt turban w/blue stone, the stem composed of two blue beads flanking center orange bead, all joined by ornate pierced gilt-metal fittings, on original round footed gilt-

Mechanical Pencil with Blackamoor Top

Caricature Pencil Sharpener

Golliwog Perfume Bottle

Blackamoor Head on Mechanical Pencil

Pencil, mechanical, gilt-metal & coral-colored beads, the top fitted w/black turbaned head of blackamoor, pierced gilt-metal fittings between the beads in the stem, Florenza, 1950s, Roger Chin Collection (ILLUS.)............. **125**

Pencil sharpener, caricature of a black man's face, traces of original red & white paint, 1/2 x 1 1/8 x 1 1/2" (ILLUS. top right).................................. **145**

Perfume bottle, glass, figural, "Golliwog de Vigny," ovoid clear frosted bottle w/paper label forming the body, wide collared rim fitted w/figural Golliwog head stopper w/fuzzy black hair, large size, Collection of Ken Leach Gallery 47 (ILLUS.) **300**

Picture frame & picture, wide flat hand-painted wooden oval frame decorated to resemble a watermelon, the oval opening enclosing a hand-colored photo of four black boys eating watermelon, late 19th - early 20th c...................................... **1,200**

Figural Native Baby Pincushion

Pincushion, figural, standing native baby holding spear & shield that forms the pincushion, 20th c. (ILLUS.) .. **45+**

Ah's 'Hand,' Mandy,' pin-up-gal, Ah keeps things nice an' neat...Gather up yo' pins an' such, an' stick 'em in ma' seat.

Figural Mammy Cardboard Pincushion

Pincushion, hanging-type, cardboard, die-cut figure of Mammy looking over her shoulder, text box above her head, cloth panel in her seat forming the pincushion (ILLUS.) **90-100**

Pincushion, silk over small paper boards, rectangular, the top printed w/scene of kneeling slave in chains above "Remember the Slave," interior w/compacted layers of cotton,

pins inserted along edges, soiled, foxed, early, 2 x 3"...................... **425-450**

Mammy Pincushion-Tape Measure

Pincushion-tape measure, cloth, figural, model of a black Mammy, red dress w/tiny white dots forming pincushion base w/tape measure, white apron & red kerchief, w/original cardboard box printed in black & red on white, Japan, ca. 1930s, mint in box, 5" h. (ILLUS.) **71**

Figural Pottery Black Man Pitcher

Pitcher, cov., pottery, figural, stout standing black man wearing brimmed cap forming the cover, his open mouth forming the spout, the cap, jacket & cravat in yellow w/his face & vest touched w/brown glaze, a drippy green glaze on his pants, black shoes, on thin oval base, England, early 19th c., Collection of John Walker Antiques & Objets de Vertu (ILLUS.) .... **1,800+**

Pitcher, earthenware, tankard-type, transfer-printed scenes titled "The Wren's Nest - The Home of Uncle Remus, Atlanta, Ga." & "A Georgia Cotton Field," also marked "Seventh Annual Convention Railway Mail Association, Atlanta, Ga. June 1909," Ridgways, England, 12 1/2" h.................................. **300-350**

Early Josephine Baker Tray

Serving tray, round, large photo of Josephine Baker shown in her famous banana costume at the Follies Bergere, Paris, 1920s, 12" d. (ILLUS.) **500**

Sign, "Antiques," figural, relief-molded figure of black man holding rectangular metal sign in front of him w/advertising, colorful old repaint, ca. 1940, several small old repairs, 4' 5 1/2" h...................................... **450-500**

Sign, "Elijah Cook," figural, carved & painted wood, finely carved standing figure of black man holding bunch of cigars in one hand & striped bat in other, atop a tall platform base painted w/"Elijah Cook - Barber - Cigars 5¢," figure wearing green pants & tan shirt, lettering in red & blue on light green ground, minor fading, scratches & paint chips, ca. 1940s-50s, 15 1/2 x 20 1/2", 5' 1" h. **1,425-1,450**

Rare Electric Theatre Segregation Sign

Sign, segregation-type, electrical neon, reads "Colored Seats Balcony [sic]," ca. 1940s, very rare (ILLUS.). **1,000**

Sign, segregation-type, "Rest Rooms," placed inside a lighted glass box over the door of the rest room, 12" l. (ILLUS. below top with other Rest Rooms sign)..................... **350**

Sign, segregation-type, "Rest Rooms," placed inside a lighted glass box over the door of the rest room, 17" l. (ILLUS. below bottom with other Rest Rooms sign) **600**

Two Segregation Rest Rooms Signs

Two Porcelain on Metal Segregation Rest Room Signs

Signs, segregation-type, porcelain on metal, for rest rooms, one reading "White Men," other reading "Colored Men," from Texas, 1930s, some edge chipping, 10" l., each (ILLUS. of two) **200**

Soap dish, cast iron, figural Mammy...... **200**

Enameled Sterling Souvenir Spoon

Copper Native Head Spoon Rest

Spoon rest, copper, stylized model of African native's head w/long ringed neck & ring earring, mid-20th c. (ILLUS.)........... **90**

Spoon, souvenir-type, sterling silver & enamel, the top of the fancy handle enameled in color w/head of black man eating slice of watermelon, the bowl engraved "Augusta, Ga.," ca. 1900, 4" l. (ILLUS. left) **431**

Spoon, sterling silver, figural black boy's head on handle, enameled watermelon in bowl, small size.... **250-275**

Mammy & Black Man Head Stamp Pad Holders

Fine Venetian Carved Blackamoors

Stamp moistening pad holder, ceramic, grotesque caricature figural of Mammy head w/wide open mouth forming the dish to hold the wetting pad, matching male head holder, early 20th c., ca. 1950s, each (ILLUS. of both bottom previous page) **350**

Stands, carved, ebonized & gilded wood, the base carved as full-figure kneeling blackamoor boy wearing short breeches carved to simulate woven grass & fitted w/painted mother-of-pearl eyes, each figure supporting a round top w/gilded chain border, figure on carved tasselled cushion, Venice, Italy, 19th c., 11 1/4" d., 21" h., pr. (ILLUS. top of page) **6,900**

Statue, copper over plaster, depicting young black man in contemplative mood sitting on tree stump, wearing jacket, pants, scarf & suspenders, "Virginia Blend" written on base, early 20th c., 9" h. **225-250**

Vase, china, cylindrical tapering at the bottom to a flared foot, hand-painted decoration of black banjo player holding straw hat, high collared jacket & striped pants, geometric bands at top & bottom edges, Union Porcelain Works, black mark "UPW," American, 19th c., 3 1/2" d., 7" h. .... **2,750+**

Figural Blackamoor Vase

Vase, figure of Blackamoor, Abingdon Pottery, No. 497D, 7 1/2" h. (ILLUS.) ... **150**

Fine Figural Majolica Vases

Vases, majolica, figural, North African boy w/cap & blue-striped robe holds basket under one arm & stands in front of large leaf cluster vase w/pink blossoms, matching girl in striped red & yellow dress & blue & white head kerchief holding basket aloft, on molded stump-form rounded base, 19th c., 11 3/4" h., pr. (ILLUS., above)......... **700+**

Rare French Porcelain Mantel Vases with Uncle Tom's Cabin Figures

Vienna Bronze of Blackamoor on Rug

Vases, mantel-type, porcelain, upright ruffled & fanned form above large scrolls & leaves all w/heavy gilt trim, each mounted at the bottom front w/a white figure group, one depicting "Uncle Tom and Little Eva in a Bower," the other "Eliza and Her Baby on the Ice Floe," Paris, third quarter 19th c., 11" h., pr. (ILLUS. bottom previous page) **3,220**

Vienna bronze, figure of seated blackamoor on woven rug w/footed cooking platform w/two copper-colored pots, a brass-colored cup & tray resting on rug, all decorated in polychrome, signed "Bergmann," Austria, late 19th c., Collection of John Walker Antiques & Objets de Vertu (ILLUS. above) .... **1,500+**

Vienna bronzes, series of three groups, each w/black man & black woman seated on bench, in the first he caresses her face, in the second she pulls away & in the third he appears to be holding her down & ready to stab her w/a dagger, polychrome decoration, Austria, late 19th c., Collection of John Walker Antiques & Objets de Vertu, set of three (ILLUS. below) .... **1,500+**

Three Vienna Bronze Groups

Walking Stick with Finely Carved Head

Walking stick, carved ebony, the handle finely carved w/the head of grinning black man wearing a link silver chain necklace, an elephant ivory ring collar separating the top from the lower ebony shaft ending in an ivory tip, found in England, ca. 1890, overall 35 1/2" l. (ILLUS. of part left) **784**

— Chapter 6 —
JEWELRY

Dress clip, bust of native w/ornate headdress & wide collar decorated w/cabochons of coral, lapis, turquoise & ivory, unmarked, 2 1/2" h. ... **$125**

Dress clip, figure of standing native holding black & gold-striped flag, gilt-metal hat & body set w/rhinestones, unmarked .... **60+**

Earrings, Bakelite, "Josephine Baker" face in profile w/gold earrings, pr. .. **100+**

Earrings, brass, native African woman w/tiny coolie-type hat, large grotesque lips, pr. .... **175+**

Earrings, sterling silver, long African mask, pierced design, 1940s, 2 1/2" l., pr....................................... **50-75**

Josephine Baker-style Necklace Figure

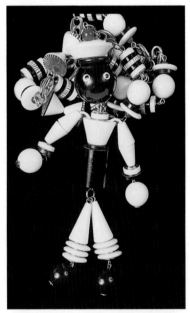

Black Sailor Figural Bead Necklace

Necklace, manipulated beads, figural, black sailor in white & black suit w/white & blue cap w/red button finial, black, white & red-striped beads forming the chain, hand-painted trim (ILLUS.) .... **250+**

Necklace, manipulated beads, figural, stylized figure of Josephine Baker-style dancer w/banana dress & trim (ILLUS. top next column) .... **250+**

Native Girl Dancer Bead Necklace

Necklace, manipulated beads, figural, stylized figure of native girl dancer w/row of colored beads forming her dress & fruit-filled hat a la Carmen Miranda, hand-painted trim (ILLUS.) . **250+**

Pin, African mask, black-painted gold metal w/gold bead drops, Collection of Roger Chin **75**

Pin, blackamoor bust, enameled sterling silver, gilt turban set w/rhinestones & wide gilt collar set w/large purple rhinestones, 1940s, Collection of Caroline & Mark Craig.............. **150**

Pin, blackamoor bust, painted gilt-metal, black & white turban trimmed w/red & clear rhinestones, pink & green rhinestone bands flanking large opal-like stone in the center of his chest, a teardrop pearl suspended at the bottom, unmarked.................. **75**

Pin, blackamoor head, enameled metal in black w/gold headdress & earrings & emerald glass eyes, unmarked, tiny, 1 1/2" l. .... **50+**

Pin, blackamoor head, facing right, gilt-metal turban & collar set w/rhinestones & large green jade nugget in turban, gold ring earring, HAR, 1950s, Collection of Roger Chin **150**

Pin, blackamoor head, gilt-metal turban trimmed w/bands of colored rhinestones, gilt-metal ring earrings, Boucher, 1960s, Collection of Roger Chin **200**

Pin, blackamoor head, metal & rhinestone, wearing turban enameled in red, white & blue, unsigned, 2" l. ..... **150+**

Pin, brass, African mask w/glass rubies & faux pearls, 2 3/4" l. .... **125+**

Pin, carved wood & plastic fiber head of native w/long pigtail ending in orange bead, ca. 1940s, Collection of Ken Leach Gallery **300**

Pin, carved wooden bust of native woman w/long beaded drop earrings, rope on hair & on neck, 4 1/2" l. .... **150+**

Pin, carved wooden face w/red exaggerated lips & clear Bakelite hair, exceptional Art Deco piece............... **250+**

Pin, ceramic, blackamoor head, green face & yellow turban, 3" h................. **150+**

Pin, figural, alligator suspending a native's head, flattened acrylic-like plastic cut-out & painted in brown, black, white & red............................... **50+**

Pin, folk art doll design, black knitted arms & head w/sewn features & pale blue kerchief, blue ribbon & red & black printed cloth dress, handmade, w/safety pin, 1 1/4" h. .... **15+**

Pin, head of native man, enameled gilt-metal, black face w/gold lips, eyes & hair & white trim, the wide curved necklace set w/almond-shaped green stones alternating w/pearl beads, unmarked, 2" h.......... **90+**

Pin, head of native woman, enameled gilt-metal, the tall pointed headdress trimmed w/rhinestones & a band of faux pearls, the gilt-metal torso trimmed w/rhinestones & central pearl, gold ring earrings, marked "PAM" **90**

Pin, Josephine Baker dancing figure, pot metal w/enamel, stylized figure in leather costume decorated w/red, white & gold, Blumenthal, 1930s, Collection of Roger Chin .... **350+**

Josephine Baker Head & Bananas Pin

Pin, Josephine Baker head, black ceramic head w/clear Lucite headdress of banana-shaped beads held by gilt-metal wire, Leo Glass, 1930s-40s, Collection of Caroline & Mark Craig (ILLUS. bottom previous page) .... **650+**

Smiling Josephine Baker Head Pin

Pin, Josephine Baker head, flattened black plastic w/red bobbed hair & lips all set w/rhinestones (ILLUS.) **165**

Pin, lacquered wood, African native mask-style head w/huge pierced lips, 5" l. .... **200+**

Pin, metal w/enamel & stones, seated black girl w/harp, marked "Coro" ...... **100+**

Pin, model of a hand, black Bakelite, the slender hand w/long red fingernails & wearing rhinestone-set ring & gilt-metal rhinestone-set bracelet w/large emerald green glass stone, 2 1/4" l. .... **125+**

Pin, native African man, mask-type in wood w/glass eyes, approximately 5" l. .... **150+**

Pin, native dancer, silver & enamel, Moderne style, 1950s, Collection of Roger Chin .... **40+**

Pin, native woman's head in profile, amber Bakelite head wearing gilt-metal high headdress w/band of green stones, Collection of Eve Savitt .... **300+**

Bakelite Sailor Pin

Pin, sailor figure, painted Bakelite, ivory-colored w/blue trim & painted red lips & white eyes, jointed at the waist w/a pin, 3 1/4" h. (ILLUS.).. **150-200**

Pin, sterling silver, blackamoor w/turban & robes, 1940s, 3 1/2" h. **100**

Pin, two-tone metal, African mask in brass w/sunburst headdress of copper, 3 1/2" l. .... **100+**

Pin and earring set, Black Sailors, paint over wood, molded ceramic turquoise, red & ochre w/details in copper wire, the set .... **150+**

Pin and earring set, sterling silver, jade & onyx, head w/huge turban, matching jade earrings, the set .... **150+**

Pins, black band members, enameled chrome & Bakelite, each stylized curved musician holding a red Bakelite instrument, 1930s, rare set, Collection of Roger Chin, the set (ILLUS. top next page) **750-1,000**

Bakelite Black Musicians Pin Set

Pins, black Mammy heads, plastic, one w/painted red kerchief, the other w/blue kerchief, each 1 1/2" h., each .... **115+**

Pins, trembler-type, native band members, painted metal, each w/square openwork frame sur-rounding stylized stick-type figure, one playing drums, one an accordion, one a bass fiddle & one a pair of maracas, each in black w/white trim, set of four, each (ILLUS. of one below).. **200**

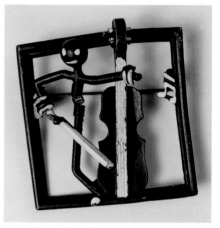

Native Band Member Pin from Set

Stickpin, figure of black bellhop, Bakelite w/gilt-metal hat & pin, bead hands & feet, painted red vest & painted facial features **85-120**

— Chapter 7 —
KITCHEN COLLECTIBLES

Large Group of Aunt Jemima Collectibles

Box, cardboard, "Aunt Jemima Pancake Flour," early image of Aunt Jemima on red background, ca. 1926, 1 lb., 4 oz. size (ILLUS. back row center with other Aunt Jemima collectibles) **$300**

Box, cardboard, "Aunt Jemima Ready-Mix Wheat and Corn Flour," smiling image of Aunt Jemima against yellow background, 1 lb. 4 oz. size (ILLUS. far right with other Aunt Jemima collectibles).................. **200**

Box, cardboard, sample size, "Aunt Jemima Buckwheat, Corn & Wheat Flour," early image of Aunt Jemima against yellow background, 4 oz. (ILLUS. far right with other Aunt Jemima collectibles)................... **250-300**

Polka Dot Mammy Butter Dish & Grease Jar

Rare Polka Dot Mammy Candy Dish

Butter dish, cov., ceramic, domed cover in the shape of a Polka Dot Mammy, part of a larger set, Japan, ca. 1940s (ILLUS. bottom of previous page right with grease jar) ... **800**

Candy dish, cov., ceramic, head of Polka Dot Mammy, Japan, ca. 1940s (ILLUS. left) **1,250**

Condiment set: cov. condiment jar & salt & pepper shakers; bisque, each piece finely molded & realistically painted as the head of a black child, on a long oval orange tray, Germany, early 20th c., each 2" h., the set (ILLUS., below)............................ **250-350**

Fine German Bisque Figural Condiment Set

Condiment Set with Natives & Native Head

Natives & Hut Condiment Set on Tray

Condiment set: mustard jar & salt & pepper shakers; ceramic, modeled as a pair of reclining African natives forming the shakers & flanking a large native head-form mustard jar w/the tongue forming the spoon, all resting on oblong fitted tray, Japan, ca. 1950s, 3" h., the set (ILLUS. bottom previous page).... **350**

Condiment set: mustard jar & salt & pepper shakers; ceramic, modeled as two African native figures forming the shakers flanking a native hut forming the mustard jar, resting on green-trimmed rectangular tray, Japan, ca. late 1940s - early 1950s, the set (ILLUS. top of page)........ **150-200**

Condiment set: mustard, salt & pepper; ceramic, modeled as stylized African native head w/bulging removable eyes, the left eye forming cover for mustard compartment w/small spoon, right eye forming pepper shaker, wide open dished mouth to hold salt for hand-sprinkling, rare, the set (ILLUS. below)...... **600**

Native Head Condiment Set

Mammy Pushing Cart Condiment Set

Pieces From a Larger Condiment Set

Condiment set: oil & vinegar cruets & salt & pepper shakers; ceramic, figural, modeled as small black Mammy wearing long red dress, white kerchief, shawl & apron & pushing large boat-shaped basketweave cart trimmed w/large strawberry, the round berry-painted containers held in the cart, Japan, ca. 1950s, cart 1 1/2 x 7 1/2", the set (ILLUS. bottom previous page) .... **400+**

Condiment set: salt & pepper, boat-shaped double spout creamer & oblong tray; ceramic, each piece in white decorated w/young dancing black woman wearing blue & white dotted dress, white apron & yellow kerchief, part of a larger set including cup & saucer, sugar bowl & other condiment pieces, the complete set (ILLUS. of part above) **450**

Condiment set: vinegar & oil containers & salt & pepper shakers; ceramic, figural, modeled as black family w/mother & father holding oil & vinegar & the boy & girl forming salt & pepper shakers, brightly painted, fitted on original wire rack, Japan, ca. 1950s, the set (ILLUS. below) **400-500**

Black Family Figural Condiment Set

"Dixie Dishes" Cookbook

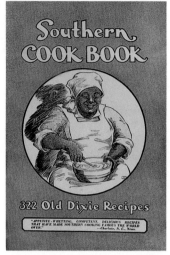

"Southern Cook Book" from 1939

Cookbook, "Dixie Dishes," by Marion W. Flexner, 1941, dark red cloth covers w/bust of black Mammy, 7 3/4" h. (ILLUS.) **50**

Cookbook, "Southern Cook Book - 322 Old Dixie Recipes," by Lillie Lustig, Claire Sondheim & Sarah Rensel, brown & white paper covers w/vignette of black cook stirring bowl, 1939 (ILLUS. top right)....... **50**

Cookie jar, ceramic, figural, full-figure Mammy w/basketweave handle, Weller lookalike, Maruhon Ware, Japan (ILLUS. back row second from right with other Maruhon Ware pieces, page 148)........................... **2,500**

Cookie jar, figural hard plastic, premium from Quaker Oats Co., F & F Mold and Die Works, 1951 (ILLUS. back row far right with other Aunt Jemima collectibles, page 139)... **450-600**

Cookie jar, figural soft plastic, premium from Quaker Oats Co. (ILLUS. back row far left with other Aunt Jemima collectibles, page 139)... **250-350**

Creamer, bisque, figural bust of smiling black boy, naturalistic coloring, Germany, ca. 1920s (ILLUS. center with figural sugar bowls, below) **500**

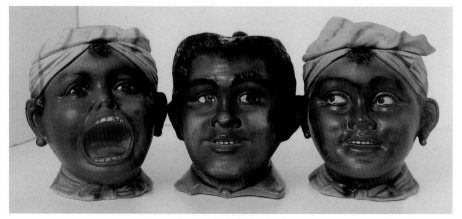

Figural Bisque Creamer & Sugar Bowls

Polka Dot Mammy Creamer, Sugar & Teapot

Creamer, ceramic, figural Polka Dot Mammy w/plaid apron, loop handles (ILLUS. front right with sugar bowl & teapot, above) **800**

Dish Towel with Black Girl

Dish towel, embroidered & painted cloth, color image of small black girl w/large slice of watermelon, edge fringe, ca. 1940s-50s, 30" l. (ILLUS.) **66**

Dish Towel with Banjo Player & Kids

Dish towel, linen, color-printed design of black man seated in front of cabin playing banjo while two children dance, 1940s (ILLUS.) **45**

Dish Towel with Black Children Design

Dish towel, linen, color-printed design of group of black children sitting & eating watermelon, cotton & blossom vining border & blue border bands, 1940s (ILLUS., above) **65**

Dish towel or pot holder racks, figural, composition or plaster-of-Paris, a black girl wearing large red ribbon & white dress & a black boy dressed as chef, ca. 1930-50, each (ILLUS. of both below) **55**

Drinking glasses, ceramic, each w/different semi-nude relief-molded native woman, possibly one of a kind, artist-signed "ALEX," the set (ILLUS. top of next page) **300**

Grease jar, cov., ceramic, modeled in the shape of a Polka Dot Mammy, part of a larger set, Japan, ca. 1940s (ILLUS. left with butter dish, bottom of page 139) **800**

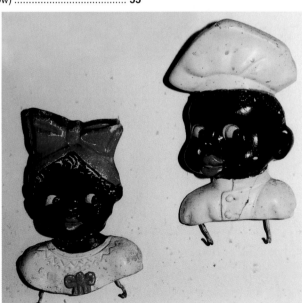

Two Figural Dish Towel Racks

Drinking Glasses with Native Women

Rare Aunt Jemima Griddle & Kitchen Collectibles

Rare Porcelain Figural Juice Reamer

Griddle, authentic Aunt Jemima promotional model, red metal (ILLUS. with a variety of Aunt Jemima kitchen collectibles previous page) **2,200-2,500**

Juice reamer, porcelain, figural, a shallow leaf-shaped dish w/loop end handle centered by the head of black man wearing pointed reamer hat, Germany, ca. 1900 (ILLUS., above) . **1,200**

Match holder, double-style, figural Polka Dot Mammy at top, part of a matching set of pieces, Japan, ca. 1940s (ILLUS. left with single match holder, right).. **600**

Match holder, single-style, figural Polka Dot Mammy at top, part of a matching set of pieces, Japan, ca.

1940s (ILLUS. below right with double match holder)................................ **450**

Two Polka Dot Mammy Match Holders

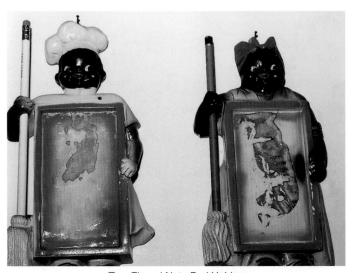

Two Figural Note Pad Holders

Note pad holders, figural composition or plaster-of-Paris, one a standing chef holding pencil forming a broom handle, a large indented red rectangular panel for holding the pad in front of his body, & one a black standing Mammy w/red kerchief & green & yellow dress also holding pencil w/broom end & w/an indented panel matching the one on the chef, ca. 1935-55, each (ILLUS. of both previous page) **100**

Oil & vinegar bottle, majolica, figural standing black Mammy, large kerchief on her head, Austria, ca. 1950s, 11 3/4" h. (ILLUS. right) **450**

Pitcher, cov., milk, ceramic, Weller lookalike Mammy figure w/her red kerchiefed head forming the cover, wearing white & red plaid dress w/large red-dotted white apron, Maruhon Ware, Japan (ILLUS. second from left with other Maruhon Ware pieces bottom of page)........... **1,200**

Pitcher, cov., water, ceramic, Weller lookalike Mammy figure w/her white kerchiefed head forming the cover, wearing white & blue plaid dress w/large blue-dotted white apron, Maruhon Ware, Japan (ILLUS. below back row far left with other Maruhon Ware pieces) **1,000**

Large Mammy Oil & Vinegar Bottle

Grouping of Ceramic Mahuron Ware Kitchen Pieces

Two Figural Black Man Water Pitchers

Pitcher, water, ceramic, figural standing black man w/wide smile on his dark black face, hands in pockets, blue hat rim, white jacket & black pants w/red shoes showing, marked "Made in Mexico- Aldana," ca. 1960s, 11" h. (ILLUS. above left with matching pitcher)........................ **700**

Pitcher, water, ceramic, figural standing black man w/wide smile on his brown face, hands in pockets, blue hat rim, white jacket & black pants w/red shoes showing, marked "Made in Mexico - Aldana," ca. 1960s, 11" h. (ILLUS. above right with matching pitcher) **700**

Pitchers, water, ceramic, caricature heads of smiling black woman & man, each (ILLUS. of both below)..... **700**

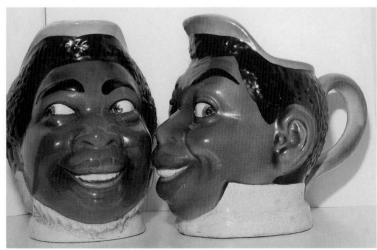

Rare Black Man & Woman Pitchers

Soldier Crap Shooters Salt & Peppers

Planter, figural, ceramic, rectangular planter molded to resemble brick wall, an excited black boy in front standing beside pair of dice, front border printed "Come Seven," Japan, ca. 1940s (ILLUS. right with matching salt & pepper shakers, page 154) **125**

Salt & pepper shakers, ceramic, figural black World War II soldiers kneeling & shooting craps, comes w/a set of ivory dice, ca. 1940s, figures each 6 1/2" l., pr. (ILLUS.).......... **250**

Salt & pepper shakers, ceramic, figural, Chef & Mammy, matches the cookie jar, Enesco, ca. 1960, pr.......... **85**

Salt & pepper shakers, ceramic, figural, exaggerated head of African woman w/red lips, Japan, ca. 1940, pr. (ILLUS. below) **125**

African Woman Head Salt & Peppers

Six Shaker Sets of Boys & Vegetables

Salt & pepper shakers, ceramic, figural, group of six sets, each set featuring a native boy astride a different vegetable including carrot, eggplant, corn, string bean, cabbage & cucumber, Japan, ca. 1950s, each set (ILLUS. of all six) ... **100+**

Salt & pepper shakers, ceramic, figural, half-length portrait of black man wearing yellow top hat, red cravat & black coat & half-length black Mammy wearing red & black kerchief & shawl over yellow dress, Germany, pre-World War II, 3 1/4" h., pr. (ILLUS. below) **250-300**

Early German Figural Ceramic Shakers

Rare Babies in Tubs Salt & Pepper Shakers

Polka Dot Mammy Salt & Peppers

Salt & pepper shakers, ceramic, figural, modeled as black babies
seated in round washtubs, Japan,
1950s, rare set, 2 3/4" h., pr.
(ILLUS. bottom previous page)......... **250**

Salt & pepper shakers, ceramic, figural, one shaker a black boy, a watermelon slice forming the other
shaker, Japan, pr. **95**

Salt & pepper shakers, ceramic, figural, Polka Dot Mammy standing
w/her hands clasped at the front,
her dark face wrinkled, wearing
kerchief & polka dot dress & plaid
apron, orange kerchief, brown &
blue polka dots & plaid, stamped
"Mammy" in the mold by the pottery, Japan, ca. 1940s, 5" h., pr.
(ILLUS. top of page).......................... **450**

Salt & pepper shakers, ceramic, figural, standing black Chef holding
trays, each w/large watermelon
wedge forming a shaker, marked
"Japan," ca. 1950s, 3" h., the set
(ILLUS. right) **300**

Chef & Watermelon Shaker Set

Salt & pepper shakers, ceramic, figural, standing black Chef & Mammy,
each holding flower-decorated cylinder in each arm, each cylinder w/re-
movable shaker, unmarked, 4 3/4" h.,
the two sets (ILLUS. top next page) **500**

Chef & Mammy Floral Shaker Sets

Chef & Mammy Shaker Sets

Salt & pepper shakers, figural, ceramic, standing black Chef & Mammy, he holding round cylinders w/removable shakers & she holding square boxes w/removable square shakers, Japan, ca. 1950s, the two sets (ILLUS. of the pair, above) **500**

Salt & pepper shakers, figural, ceramic, standing black Chef w/pipe in mouth & angry expression holding a rolling pin & frying pan, & matching Mammy wearing yellow kerchief & holding colorful duck, Japan, 1950s, 5" h., pr. (ILLUS. right) **175-200**

Angry-looking Chef & Mammy Shakers

Chef & Mammy with Spoon Shakers

Salt & pepper shakers, figural, ceramic, standing black chef wearing striped shirt, white hat & gold-dotted apron & holding gold spoon & a matching Mammy wearing blue kerchief, red & white dress & gold-trimmed apron & spoon, Japan, ca. 1950s, 3" h., pr. (ILLUS. above) ... **85-100**

Salt & pepper shakers, figural, ceramic, two little black boys shooting dice, each figure forming a shaker, on oblong tray w/dice between them, Japan, ca. 1940s, the set (ILLUS. left with matching planter below) **150**

Dice Boy Shakers on Tray & Matching Planter

Black Valentine Couple Shakers

Salt & pepper shakers, figural, ceramic, Valentine couple, black woman w/grey hair standing wearing white apron w/red trim, black man w/grey hair standing wearing green shirt & pale yellow pants & holding large red heart Valentine, Japan, 1950s, 5" h., pr. (ILLUS. left) **150-175**

Salt & pepper shakers, hard plastic, figural Aunt Jemima & Uncle Mose, F. & F. Mold & Die Works, 3 1/2" h. pr. .... **65+**

Salt & pepper shakers, hard plastic, figural Aunt Jemima & Uncle Mose, F. & F. Mold & Die Works, 5 1/4" h., pr. .... **85+**

Spice Set & Rack Decorated with Black Figures

Shopping reminder peg board, plywood, red & black decoration of bust of black Mammy w/string around her finger at the top beside wording "I'se Gotta Git...," peg holes w/various groceries below, ca. 1950s (ILLUS. previous page) **75**

Pegboard with Full Figure Mammy

Shopping reminder peg board, wooden, long rectangular form, decorated w/full-length portrait of smiling black Mammy carrying a cake, wearing blue dress w/white blossoms, red & white polka dot kerchief, white apron & black shoes, "Shopping Reminder" at top above a bordered rectangle w/peg holes & list of various groceries, ca. 1950s (ILLUS.) **75**

Spice rack with containers, hard plastic figures of Aunt Jemima marked w/different spices, fitted in metal frame, Quaker Oats premium, F. & F. Mold and Die Company, the set (ILLUS. front row center with other Aunt Jemima collectibles, page 139) .... **1,000+**

Spice set: six cylindrical containers on wooden rack; ceramic, each container in white w/gold & silver foil label naming the spice, each w/different colored cap & each molded w/either a black Chef or Mammy decorated in color, Japan, ca. 1950s, the set (ILLUS., top of page)... **225**

Spoon rests, metal, figural w/painted color decoration, one a black Chef w/bowl & spoon, the other a black Mammy w/sad iron, Toledo Stove & Range Co., pr. (ILLUS. of both top next page) **250**

Black Chef & Black Mammy Metal Spoon Rests

Polka Dot Mammy String Holder

String holder, ceramic, head of Polka Dot Mammy, Japan, ca. 1940s (ILLUS.) **500**

Mammy with White Lips String Holder

String holder, hanging-type, ceramic, figural black Mammy head, dark brown skin w/white lips & kerchief, large size (ILLUS.).............................. **300**

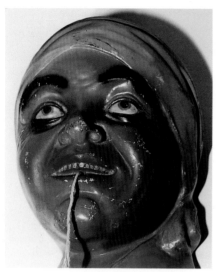

Figural Black Mammy String Holder

String holder, hanging-type, ceramic, figural black Mammy head wearing dark green kerchief, Fredericksburg Art Pottery, Fredericksburg, Ohio, ca. 1940s (ILLUS.) **350**

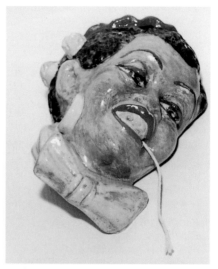

Black Man with Bow Tie String Holder

String holder, hanging-type, ceramic, figural black man's face, light brown skin & bow tie w/red lips & black & white eyes, wearing a red & white cap, ca. 1935-55 (ILLUS.) **100**

Black Man with Red Hat String Holder

String holder, hanging-type, ceramic, figural black man's face, dark black skin, smiling w/thick red lips, red pillbox hat, Fredericksburg Art Pottery, Fredericksburg, Ohio, 1939-49, 6 1/2" h. (ILLUS.) **350**

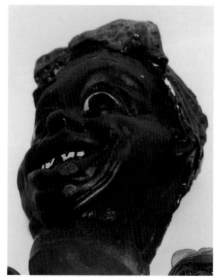

Smiling Dark Mammy String Holder

String holder, hanging-type, composition or plaster-of-Paris, figural dark black Mammy face w/painted red kerchief, lips & collar w/white teeth & black & white eyes, ca. 1930-50 (ILLUS.).............................. **250+**

Sugar bowl, cov., bisque, figural, bust of screaming black girl wearing blue-striped white kerchief, naturalistic coloring, Germany, ca. 1920s (ILLUS. left with figural girl creamer, page 143) **400**

Sugar bowl, cov., bisque, figural, bust of smiling black girl wearing blue-striped white kerchief, naturalistic coloring, Germany, ca. 1920s (ILLUS. right with figural girl creamer, page 143) **350**

Sugar bowl, cov., ceramic, figural Polka Dot Mammy w/plaid apron, loop handle (ILLUS. front left with creamer & teapot, page 144) **1,000**

Sugar bowl (or jam jar), cov., ceramic, Weller lookalike Mammy figure w/her white kerchiefed head forming the cover, wearing white & blue plaid dress w/large blue-dotted white apron, Maruhon Ware, Japan (ILLUS. front row right with other Maruhon Ware pieces, page 148) **800**

Syrup pitcher, ceramic, name of Aunt Jemima printed in red on the side, 1988 Quaker Oats premium (ILLUS. front row far left with other Aunt Jemima collectibles, page 139).......... **65+**

Syrup pitcher, cov., ceramic, figural Mammy, Weller Pottery Mammy Line, ca. 1930s, overall crazing, 6 1/2" h. (ILLUS. top right) **468**

Syrup pitcher, plastic, figural Aunt Jemima, F. & F. Mold & Die Works, Quaker Oats premium, ca. 1949.......... **85**

Weller Pottery Mammy Line Syrup

Syrup pitcher (or creamer), cov., ceramic, Weller lookalike Mammy figure w/her red kerchiefed head forming the cover, wearing white & red plaid dress w/large red-dotted white apron, Maruhon Ware, Japan (ILLUS. front row left with other Maruhon Ware pieces, page 148) **800**

Tea set: cov. teapot, cov. sugar bowl & creamer; ceramic, teapot a figural Mammy head, the sugar & creamer figural children's heads, faces glazed in dark brown w/black hair & wearing white caps, Japan, ca. 1945-55, the set (ILLUS. below) **250**

Figural Tea Set with Brown Faces

Figural Tea Set with Black Faces

Tea set: cov. teapot, cov. sugar bowl & creamer; ceramic, teapot a figural Mammy head, the sugar & creamer figural children's heads, faces glazed in black w/tan hair & wearing white caps, matches a set w/dark brown faces, Japan, ca. 1945-55, the set (ILLUS. above) **250**

marked "USA," overall crazing, 8" l., 8" h. (ILLUS.) **94**

Teapot, cov., ceramic, figural Polka Dot Mammy w/plaid apron, loop handle (ILLUS. back center with creamer & sugar bowl, page 144) ... **2,000**

Rare Polka Dot Mammy Teapot

Teapot, cov., ceramic, head of Polka Dot Mammy, Japan, ca. 1940s (ILLUS.) **1,000**

Teapot, cov., ceramic, Weller looka-like Mammy figure w/her red ker-chiefed head forming the cover, wearing white & red plaid dress w/large red-dotted white apron, Maruhon Ware, Japan (ILLUS. back row far right with other Maruhon Ware pieces, page 148) **1,200**

Colorful Black Mammy Teapot

Teapot, cov., ceramic, figural, mod-eled as black Mammy w/the base formed by her wide green skirt & apron, holding a long red wedge of watermelon at front, yellow blouse & white striped kerchief, bottom

Figural Black Man Water Set

Water set: figural pitcher & head-shaped mugs; ceramic, figural standing black man w/wide smile on his brown face, hands in pockets, blue hat rim, white jacket & black pants w/red shoes showing, four matching mugs, marked "Made in Mexico - Aldana," ca. 1960s, pitcher 11" h., the set (ILLUS.)................ **1,500**

— Chapter 8 —
MUSIC & RECORDS

Catalog, "Decca Race Records," paper, small photographs of various black artists, reads "Blues Singing, Blues Dance, Hot Dance, Sacred Preaching," artists listed alphabetically by category, 1940, 24 pages, 6 x 9" (some cover dings & soil) **$95**

Concert program, "The Genius of Ray Charles," paper, produced by ABC-Paramount for his tour promoting the album "Modern Sounds in Country & Western Music," many photos & a biography, cover w/orange ink, 20 pages, 9 x 12" (front cover slightly bent, slight cover wear & slight soil on pages) **150**

Phonograph record, "Night Watchman Blues - What' Wrong with Me," by Big Bill, Okeh Records, No. 6705 (light wear, minor scratches) **18**

Phonograph record, "Training Camp Blues - Sugar Babe Blues," by Roosevelt Sykes aka "The Honey Dipper," Okah Records, No. 6709 (some wear & scratches) **18**

Poster, cardboard, "Emory Howard and his Peerless Syncopators," photo illustration of the band, in the upper left corner "The Six '6' Vikings," dated "Thursday Feb. 27th - Elks New Ball Room Monongahela," Pennsylvania, 1920s, 10 1/2 x 14" (small tear at top edge) **90**

Program, "The Biggest Show of Stars for '57," paper, fall program for touring rock & roll show, includes Fats Domino, Clyde McPhatter, LaVern Baker, Frankie Lymon, Chuck Berry, Buddy Holly & the Crickets & more, blue, red, gold & black cover, many photos & biographies of the artists, 24 pages, 9 x 12" (cover slightly rubbed, pages slightly browned) **100**

Program, "The Biggest Show of Stars for '58," paper, spring program for touring rock & roll show, includes Sam Cooke, Paul Anka, LaVern Baker, Clyde McPhatter, The Silhouettes & many others, bust photos on the cover, cover in blue, red, yellow & black, inside photos & biographies, 24 pages, 9 x 12" (minor spine scuffs)... **100**

Program, "The Biggest Show of Stars for '59," paper, spring program w/all-black cast, including Lloyd Price, The Coasters, The Chantels, Wade Flemons, The Crests, Bo Diddley & many others, photos of the stars on the cover & inside, gold & orange cover, 24 pages, 9 x 12" **100**

Program, "The Biggest Show of Stars for '61," paper, spring program w/all-black cast, including The Shells, Chuck Jackson, The Drifters, Bo Diddley, The Shirelles, Chubby Checker & many others, stars' photos on the cover & inside, 24 pages, 9 1/2 x 12 1/4" **125**

Josephine Baker 45 RPM Record

Record, "Josephine Baker," 45 rpm, RCA, includes four songs, original sleeve w/photo of Josephine Baker in costume, ca. 1960s (ILLUS.) **95**

Record album, "Freedom In The Air - Albany, Georgia," 33 1/3 rpm, documentary on Albany, Georgia, in 1961-62, produced by Alan Lomax & Guy Carawan, manufactured by SNCC, extensive liner notes, cover split halfway along top edge, light edge foxing..... **61**

Record album, "Negro Sinful Songs by Lead Belly," Musicraft Album 31, five 78 rpms, cover photo of black person picking cotton w/cabin in background, ca. 1940s (cover worn, spine split & soiled, records excellent)... **435**

Rock poster, B.B. King, Pleasure
Pier, Galveston, Texas, 1955 ..... **100-150**

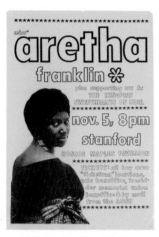

1970s Aretha Franklin Poster

Rock poster, concert-type, "Aretha
Franklin," cardboard w/yellow background print in black w/a large half-
length photo of the star, early 1970s
concert in Palo Alto, California, sta-
ple holes & corner wear, 11 x 17"
(ILLUS.) **575**

Diana Ross & The Supremes Poster

Rock poster, concert-type, "Diana
Ross & the Supremes," cardboard
w/a shaded yellow to orange to
blue background, photo of the
group & wording in black, 1960s
concert in San Diego, 13 1/2 x 22"
(ILLUS.) **3,031**

Colorful Early James Brown Poster

Rock poster, concert-type, "The Fabulous James Brown," cardboard
printed in orange, yellow, white,
blue & black, James Brown head
photo, 1966 concert in Providence,
Rhode Island, 22 x 28" (ILLUS.)...... **3,699**

Rock poster, Diana Ross & the Su-
premes, in yellow, orange & blue
w/photo of the Supremes, reads
"Diana Ross - & the Supremes -
Sun. Aug. 17 - 8:30 p.m. - Sports
Arena" etc., 1960s, 14 x 22" **750-775**

Rock poster, Howlin' Wolf, black &
yellow, at the Matrix, 1967........... **150-200**

Rock poster, Ike and Tina Turner Revue, Oakland Auditorium, San Francisco, California, Friday, January
13, 1967 .... **300-500**

Rock poster, Jackie Wilson, at the
Evergreen Ballroom, Olympia,
Washington, October 13, 1963.... **300-500**

Rock poster, James Brown, "Mr. Dy-
namite," at the Apollo Theatre, New
York, 1966.................................. **450-500**

Rock poster, James Brown, "Sex, Power and Love," The Civic Auditorium,
San Francisco, October 23, 1971 ... **250-350**

Rock poster, Jimi Hendrix, for concerts
at the Fillmore Auditorium & Winter-
land in San Francisco, February 14,
1968, features Rick Griffin's flying
eyeball, Bill Graham, No. 105, first
printing, 14 x 21 1/2".............. **1,000-1,200**

Rock poster, Jimi Hendrix, pink & turquoise, at the Earl Warren Showgrounds, Santa Barbara, August 19, 1967 .... **350-500**

Rock poster, Lightning Hopkins, black & white, "The King of Blues," 1965.. **150-200**

Rock poster, Marvin Gaye, Sportsman Club #2, December 9, 1965 .... **250-300**

Rock poster, Otis Redding, at the Continental Club, August 21, 1967 ...... **250-300**

Rock poster, The Four Tops, The Fillmore Auditorium, San Francisco, September 27, 1966 .... **150-200**

Rock poster, The Temptations, at the Fillmore Auditorium, San Francisco, Tuesday, July 26, 1966 .... **150-200**

Sheet music, "Any Rags," large comic figure of black rag man on the cover, small vignette photo of female singer, by Thos. S. Allen, 6 pages, 1902 .... **95**

Sheet music, "Banjo-Pickaninnies," by T. Robin MacLachlan, published by Harold Flammer, Inc., New York, 1928, six pages, minor soiling **35**

Sheet music, "By the Watermelon Vine, Lindy Lou," by Thomas Allen, black comic scene of young black couple seated together against giant wedge of watermelon in watermelon patch, cover in red, green & brown, black dialect lyrics, 1904, 6 pages, 10 x 14" **120**

Sheet music, "Coons in the Cottonfield," large vignette scene of blacks dancing in cotton field, a schottische by J.W. Wheeler, cover in yellow, blue & white, 6 pages, 1898 (edge browning, few minor tears) **110**

Sheet music, "Do Nothin' Till You Hear From Me," by Duke Ellington, photo of Ellington at the piano on the cover, red & blue cover, 4 pages, 1943 (slight soiling) **125**

Sheet music, "J'ai Lu Dans Les Etoiles (I Read in the Stars)," photo of Josephine Baker, 1956 (ILLUS. top right) **125**

Josephine Baker Sheet Music

Sheet music, "Little Eva - Uncle Tom's Guardian Angel," vignette of Eva & Uncle Tom on the cover, 1852, poetry by John Greenleaf Whittier, music by Manuel Emilio, dedicated to Mrs. Harriet Beecher Stowe, published by John P. Jewett & Co. (disbound, some spine soil, minor foxing) **95**

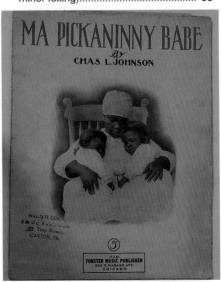

"Ma Pickaninny Babe" Sheet Music

Early Josephine Baker Sheet Music

Sheet music, "Ma Pickaninny Babe," by Chas. L. Johnson, photo of black wom-

an seated holding two black children, Foster Music Publisher, Chicago, early 20th c. (ILLUS. previous page) **125**

Sheet music, "My Little Mule and I," by Fred Lyons, large caricature picture on cover of seated black man playing banjo w/mule beside him, cabin in background, published by W.F. Shaw, 1884, some overall soiling, 10 3/4 x 14" **110**

Sheet music, "Sans Amour," cover photo of Josephine Baker, France, 1933 (ILLUS. left) **125**

Sheet music, "Slavery Days," by Harrigan & Braham, cover sketch of two black women seated flanking a basket of cotton, cover notes "song & chorus" but only a waltz inside, 6 pages, 1876, 10 x 13" (disbound, small damages) **95**

"Queen of Charcoal Alley" Sheet Music

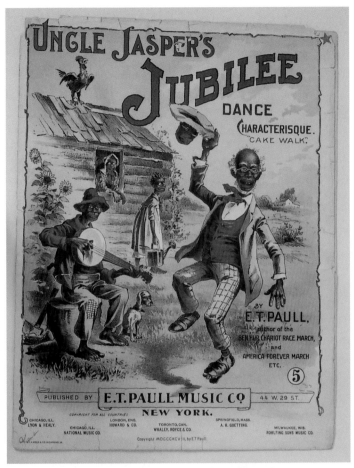

"Uncle Jasper's Jubilee" Sheet Music

Sheet music, "The Queen of Charcoal Alley," special "Supplement to the Empress Magazine, January 1901," colorful vignette of elegant black couple & their poodle framed by sunflowers, "Words by Andrew B. Sterlig - Music by Howard and Emerson" (ILLUS. bottom previous page).. **125**

Sheet music, "Uncle Jasper's Jubilee Dance - Characterisque - 'Cake Walk,'" color comic cover by E.T. Paull, E.T. Paull Music Co., New York, copyright 1898 (ILLUS. above).. **125**

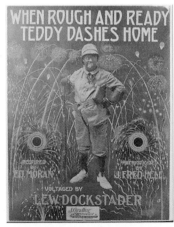

Satiric Teddy Roosevelt Sheet Music

Sheet music, "When Rough and Ready Teddy Dashes Home," tinted color cover photo of the famous minstrel Lew Dockstader dressed to resemble Teddy Roosevelt as the Great White Hunter, ca. 1910 (ILLUS. previous page) **58**

Sheet music, "You Can't Fool Me No More," by Nathan Bivins, cover w/black caricatures of angry-looking black man standing staring across at smiling young black woman who holds his hat, images centered by photograph of white singer May Ward, captioned "Dainty Little Comedienne," red & green cover, black dialect lyrics, 1900, 6 pages, 11 x 14" (very slight soil, minor wear) ... **100**

L.P. RECORDS & ORIGINAL JACKETS

All illustrated records from the Collection of Jack Peapopa of Rare Records, Teaneck, New Jersey.

Ayers (Roy), "He's coming - Roy Ayers Ubiquity," Polydor No. 5022, funk music, original pressing **100**

Miles Davis Record Album

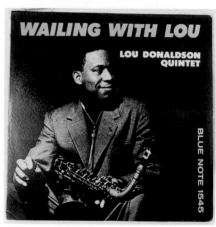

Lou Donaldson Record Album

Sonny Clark Record Album

Clark (Sonny), "Sonny's Crib - Sonny Clark - Donald Byrd Curtis Fuller John Coltrane - Paul Chambers Art Taylor, Blue Note 1576," bebop music, original pressing (ILLUS.) **550**

Davis (Miles), "Musings of Miles," Prestige No. 7007, bebop music, original pressing (ILLUS. top right) **200**

Donaldson (Lou), "Wailing With Lou - Lou Donaldson Quintet - Blue Note 1545," bebop music, original pressing (ILLUS. middle right) **475**

Kenny Drew Record Album

Drew (Kenny), "The Modernity of Kenny Drew," Norgran Records, No. MGN 1002, bebop music, original pressing (ILLUS. previous page) bottom right **150**

Curtis Fuller Record Album

Fuller (Curtis), "Curtis Fuller - New Trombone - with red kyner/hank jones/doug watkins - louis hayes/prestige 7107," bebop music, original pressing (ILLUS.) **175**

Gladys Knight & The Pips, "Anthology," Motown #792, 1974 .... **25**

Rare Dexter Gordon Record Album

Gordon (Dexter), "Dexter Blows Hot And Cool," Dootone DL 207, red vinyl, bebop music, original pressing (ILLUS.) **850**

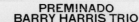

Barry Harris Record Album

Harris (Barry), "Preminado - Barry Harris Trio - with Elvin Joines, Joe Benjamin," Riverside No. 354, bebop music, original pressing (ILLUS.)........... **75**

Hartman (Johnny), "All of Me - the Debonair mr. hartman," Bethlehem BCP 6014, jazz vocal, original pressing (ILLUS. next page)................ **65**

Weldon Irvine Record Album

Irvine (Weldon), "liberated brother - weldon irvine," Nodlew Music Records, funk jazz, original pressing (ILLUS.) **200**

Johnny Hartman Record Album

Mahalia Jackson Record Album

Jackson (Mahalia), "Mahalia," Apollo No. 486, gospel music, original pressing (ILLUS. previous page) **125**

James Brown, "James Brown & His Famous Flames," King #683, 1960..... **400**

James Brown, "Please, Please, Please," King #610, 1959 .... **300**

James Brown, "Prisoner of Love," King #851, 1963.................................... **75**

James Brown, "Try Me," King #635, 1959... **300**

Rare Thad Jones Record Album

Jones (Thad), "The Magnificent Thad Jones - Blue Note 1527," bebop music, original pressing (ILLUS.) **550**

Rare Cliff Jordan Record Album

Jordan (Cliff), "Cliff Craft - Cliff Jordan - Blue Note 1582," bebop music, original pressing (ILLUS.) **600**

Martha and The Vandellas, "Come and Get These Memories," Gordy #902, 1963 .... **300**

Martha and The Vandellas, "Dance Party," Gordy #915, 1965.................... **90**

Martha and The Vandellas, "Heat Wave," Gordy #907, 1963 .... **100**

Marvin Gaye, "Greatest Hits," Tamala #252, 1964 .... **60**

Marvin Gaye, "Soulful Sounds of Marvin Gaye," Tamala #221, 1961 .... **700**

Marvin Gaye, "That Stubborn Kind of Fella," Tamala #239, 1963 .... **500**

Marvin Gaye, "When I'm Alone I Cry," Tamala #251, 1964 .... **200**

Mary Wells, "Mary Wells," Motown #600, 1961 .... **400**

Mary Wells, "The One Who Really Loves You," Motown #605, 1962....... **300**

Mary Wells, "Two Lovers," Motown #607, 1963 .... **200**

Jackie McLean Record Album

McLean (Jackie), "Jackie's Pal - introducing - Bill Hardman - Jackie McLean quintet - Mal Waldron - Paul Chambers - 'Philly' Joe Jones," Prestige No. 7068, bebop music, original pressing (ILLUS.) **425**

McLean (Jackie), "The New Tradition - presenting - jackie mclean," Ad Lib No. 6601, bebop music, original pressing (ILLUS. next page)............ **1,000**

Very Rare Jackie McLean Album

Charles Mingus Tour Record Album

Rare Lee Morgan Record Album

Mingus (Charles), "Town Hall Concert - Charles Mingus - Music Played on European Tour - '64 - featuring Charles Mingus - Eric Dolphy & Clifford Jordan - Jaki Byard - Dannie Richmond - Johnny Coles," JW No. 5005, bebop music, original pressing (ILLUS.) **175**

Morgan (Lee), "Candy - Lee Morgan - Blue Note 1590," bebop music, original pressing (ILLUS.) **750**

Oreos, "It's Too Soon To Know," Jubilee, 1954 .... **5,000**

Oreos, "What Are You Doing New Year's Eve?," Jubilee #501, 1954 ...... **500**

Charlie Parker Record Album

Parker (Charlie), "Bird at St. Nick's -
JWS - Jazz Workshop 500," bebop
music, original pressing (ILLUS.
above) **125**

Rare Charlie Parker Record Album

Parker (Charlie), "Charlie Parker -
201 - dial," Dial No. 201, bebop mu-
sic, original pressing (ILLUS.) **600**

Duke Pearson Record Album

Pearson (Duke), "Profile Duke Pearson a lyrical pianist...with a fine
sense of time and dynamics...ideas
of clarity and brightness...a flowing,
effortless swing," Blue Note No.
4022, bebop music, original press-
ing (ILLUS.) **350**

Ray Charles, "Original Ray Charles," Hollywood #504, 1959 .... **200**

Ray Charles, "Ray Charles," Atlantic #8006, 1957 .... **150**

Ray Charles, "Yes Indeed," Atlantic #8025, 1959 .... **75**

Rollins (Sonny), "Saxophone Colossus - Sonny Collins - Tommy Flanagan Doug Watkins Max Roach," Prestige No. 7079, bebop music, original pressing (ILLUS. right) **600**

Rollins (Sonny), "Sonny Rollins - Way Out West," Contemporary No. C3530, bebop music, original pressing (ILLUS. bottom of page) **75**

Smokey and the Miracles, "Bad Girls," Motown, 1959 .... **1,500**

Smokey and the Miracles, "Christmas Song," Tamala, 1963 .... **200**

Smokey and the Miracles, "Christmas With The Miracles," Tamala, 1962 .... **200**

Smokey and the Miracles, "Cooking With The Miracles," Tamala #223, 1961 .... **500**

Smokey and the Miracles, "I Care About Detroit," Tamala, 1968 .... **200**

Smokey and the Miracles, "We're The Miracles," Tamala #220, 1961 ..... **500**

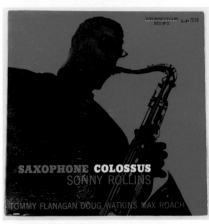

Rare Sonny Rollins Record Album

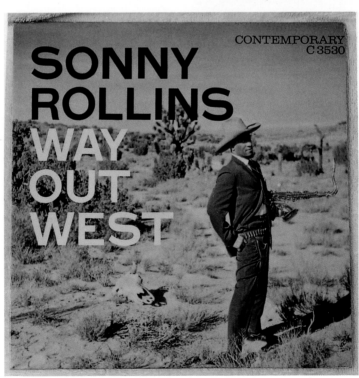

Sonny Rollins Record Album

Mal Waldron Record Album

Lem Winchester Record Album

The Drifters, "Clyde McPhatter & The Drifters," Atlantic #8003, 1957 .... **300**

The Drifters, "Rockin' & Driftin'," Atlantic #8022, 1959 .... **200**

The Drifters, "The Drifters Greatest Hits," Atlantic #8041, 1960 .... **100**

The Supremes, "I Want A Guy," Motown #1008, 1961 .... **100**

The Supremes, "Let Me Go The Right Way," Motown #1034, 1962 .... **80**

The Supremes, "Your Heart Belongs To Me," Motown #1027, 1962 .... **50**

The Temptations, "Getting Ready," Gordy #918, 1966 .... **40**

The Temptations, "Greatest Hits," Gordy #919, 1966 .... **50**

The Temptations, "Meet the Temptations," Gordy #911, 1964 .... **60**

The Temptations, "Temptations Sing Smokey," Gordy #912, 1965 .... **40**

Waldron (Mal), "Mal 2 - Prestige 7111 - Mal Waldron with - Jackie McLean, John Coltrane, Idrees Sulieman, Sahib Shihab, and Bill Hardman," Prestige No. 7111, bebop music, original pressing (ILLUS., above left) **250**

Winchester (Lem), "Winchester Special - Lem Winchester & Benny Golson," New Jazz No. 8223, bebop music, original pressing (ILLUS. above right) **100**

5 Keys, "Best of the 5 Keys," Aladdin #806, 1956 .... **40**

5 Keys, "The 5 Keys On Stage," Capitol #828, 1957 .... **700**

— Chapter 9 —

PAPER COLLECTIBLES

Autograph, Booker T. Washington (1856-1915), letter signed on Tuskegee Institute stationery, a lengthy thank you for a $100 donation (short tear in the left margin)... **$175+**

Autograph, Booker T. Washington, trimmed from letter, 2 1/4 x 5 1/4"......... **77**

Autograph, Langston Hughes, 1960 autograph of the famed poet, a key figure in the Harlem Renaissance, active in civil rights & left-wing politics, large bold signature, matted & framed w/photograph of Hughes **350**

Autograph, W.E.B. DuBois, typed letter signed on Dubois letterhead offering the editor of the Massachusetts Review a chapter from his forthcoming autobiography, clear signature in ink in another hand below "Title - a Soliloquy on Viewing My Life from the Last Decades of My First Century," dated January 4, 1960...................... **400+**

Baseball card, Billy Williams, 1961 Topps, No. 141 .... **125+**

Baseball card, Bob Gibson, 1959 Topps, No. 514 .... **275+**

Baseball card, Ernie Banks, 1954 Topps, No. 94 .... **800+**

Baseball card, Hank Aaron, 1954 Topps, No. 128 .... **750+**

1968 Topps Hank Aaron Baseball Card

Baseball card, Hank Aaron, 1968 Topps, No. 110 (ILLUS.) **75-100**

Baseball card, Jackie Robinson, 1948 Leaf, No. 79........................... **500+**

Baseball card, Jackie Robinson, 1952 Topps, No. 312...................... **750+**

Baseball card, Lou Brock, 1962 Topps, No. 387............................... **200+**

Baseball card, Reggie Jackson, 1969 Topps, No. 260............................... **200+**

Baseball card, Satchel Paige, 1948 Leaf, No. 8................................... **1,200+**

Baseball card, Satchel Paige, 1949 Bowman, No. 224........................... **600+**

Baseball card, Willie Mays, 1951 Bowman, No. 305........................ **1,200+**

Baseball card, Willie Mays, 1954 Topps, No. 90................................. **500+**

Baseball ticket, "Homestead Grays vs Philadelphia Stars," yellow card, held at Swayne Field, Toledo, Ohio, Wednesday, August 19, 1936 - 9 p.m., cost 40¢, 2 1/4 x 3 1/2" (slightly soiled) **200-250**

Book, "46th Field Artillery Brigade Pictorial History," red cloth covers, story of black U.S. Army troops commanded by white officers, includes photos and information on other black units, 1942, 9 x 12" (cover slightly worn, spine a little loose)........ **125**

Book, "Anti-Slavery in America," by Mary Stoughton Locke, Boston, Ginn & Co., history of slavery in America, 1901, paper covers w/tan wraps, 22 pp. (cover worn, fragile & almost detached, missing back cover, some page browning)..................... **55**

Book, "Harlem Shadows, The Poems of Claude McKay," Harcourt Brace, first edition, 1922, 95 pages, 5 x 7 1/2" (some cover soil)............... **150**

Book, "Scott's American Negro in the World War," salesman's sample abbreviated edition, profusely illustrated, opens w/information on selling & promoting the book, red board covers, 1919...................... **198**

Book, "Story of the John Brown Bell," produced by the John A. Rawlins Post 43, Grand Army of the Republic, photos of sights in Harpers Ferry & the bell, w/the story of John Brown, 1910, hard covers, 20 pp., 6 x 8" **39**

Book, "The Fastest Bicycle Rider in the World...," autobiography of Marshall W. "Major" Taylor, personally inscribed & dated 1929, copyright 1928 (spine loose) **440**

Book, "The Official History and Manual of the Grand United Order of Odd Fellows in America (Colored Men)," by Chas. Brooks, black cloth covers, Philadelphia, 1902, photos of English & American officers & records, 276 pages, 6 x 8 1/2" (cover worn, spine loosened, pages slightly browned & some stained) **100**

Booklet, color illustrations, cardboard, one of a black golf caddy on the fairway, another of a black boy carrying a large American flag, part of a series, booklet title unknown, American-made, ca. 1907, also found as postcards, each (ILLUS. of two below & at right) **45**

Booklet, fold-out type, each page w/color illustration of comical scenes in a series of short uncaptioned stories, marked "Printed in Germany," 1890s, book 6 x 8", each page (ILLUS. of two pages next page) **75**

Booklet, "John Brown's Expedition Reviewed - A Letter from Rev. Theodore Parker at Rome to Francis Jackson, Boston," published in Boston by The Fraternity, 1860, 20 pp., 4 5/8 x 7 1/2" **77**

Two Comical Color Booklet Illustrations

Two Pages from a German Booklet

Broadside, printed paper, "100 Negroes - For Sale - On the 3d Monday of Jan'y next, 20th...," from a plantation on "the Yellow Bluff," near Arcola, farm utensils, stocks & tracts of land also offered, for January 20, 1851, printed in Mobile, Alabama, December 18, 1850, 12 x 15 1/2" (lightly foxed, ink stains & burns, folds) .... **4,000+**

Broadside, printed paper, reward-type, "$300 REWARD - Run Away from the subscriber on August the 4th, 1 'ocl'k A.M., a negro man calling himself Randolph Jackson, about 23 years of age, copper color, five feet 8 inches, with full cheeks and thick set...," from Buena Vista, Maryland, roughly printed, browned, water stained, folds, some tears, 9 1/2 x 12" .... **1,250+**

Broadside, "Stop the Ku Klux Klan Propaganda in New York City," released by the NAACP urging the public to protest the showing of the movie "Birth of a Nation" in New York City, cream paper, ca. 1921, 9 x 13 1/2" (crudely repaired tear) **97**

Broadside, two-sided, a map of the South & promotional information printed in red & black, explains national fundraising efforts of the Freed-

man's Aid and Southern Educational Society of the Methodist Episcopal Church, ca. 1890, 26 x 30" (small tear in top margin, small splits at folds) **1,387**

Early Josephine Baker Movie Brochure

Brochure, advertising the movie "Zuzu," cover picture of a young Josephine Baker in costume, in Italian, 1920s (ILLUS.) **75**

Two Comical Cards of Black Boxers

Cards, color lithographed paper, a series of small black comical cards showing two black men wearing top hats, formal jackets & red & white striped pants involved in a boxing match, artist-signed "Ellam," marked on back "Printed in Germany," early 20th c., each card (ILLUS. of two, above) **65**

Catalog, "Denison's Minstrel and Song Catalogue," red, white & black cover w/well-dressed minstrel man,

T.S. Denison & Company, Chicago, 1907 (ILLUS. of cover & sample page top of next page) **45**

Children's book, "All About Little Black Sambo," illustrated by John B. Gruelle, black & white & color illustrations by the creator of Raggedy Ann, Cupples & Leon Company, New York, 1920s (ILLUS. of cover, title page & first page, following pages) **150**

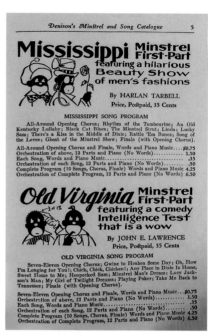

Denison's Catalog Cover & Sample Page

"All About Little Black Sambo" Pages

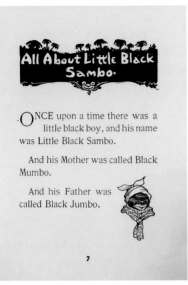

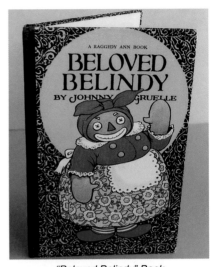

"Beloved Belindy" Book

Children's book, "Beloved Belindy,"
1926, Volland edition (ILLUS.) **160**

"All About Little Black Sambo" Page

Page from "Four & Twenty Dollies"

Children's book, "Four & Twenty Dollies," boxed hard-cover volume w/loose color-illustrated pages, various stories, illustrated by Ella Dollbear Lee, Hamming Publishing Co., copyright 1914 (ILLUS. of first page of one story in the book, previous page)... **125-150**

Rand McNally "Little Black Sambo"

Children's book, "Little Black Sambo," Rand McNally Book, hard cover, 1955, color cover, some wear (ILLUS.).. **125**

Children's book, "Pickaninny ABC - Dean's Rag Books Patented No. 39," linen-type, color pictures of black children in various poses representing letters of the alphabet, printed in England, "Patented U.S.A. Mar. 7, 1905"........................... **125**

Children's book, "The Kewpies," cardboard soft covers, w/various poems, stories & illustrations by Rose O'Neill, includes "The Kewpies and the Little Browns," after 1925 (ILLUS. of two pages bottom of page) **125-150**

Children's book, "The Story of Little Black Sambo - Told and Pictured by Helen Bannerman - The Only Edition with the Original Pictures," hard cover, 1930 (ILLUS. left, top of next page) **150**

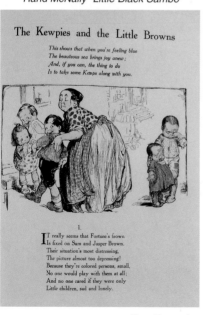

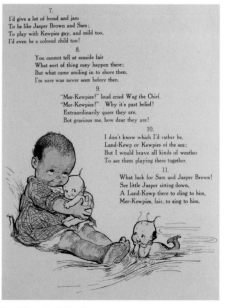

Two Pages from "The Kewpies" Book

"The Story of Little Black Sambo" Cover

Early Outcault Christmas Card

Page from "The Ten Little Mulligan Guards"

Children's book, "The Ten Little Mulligan Guards," boxed book w/color-illustrated pages, McLoughlin Brothers, New York, 1873 copyright (ILLUS. of one inside page, above) **200**

Children's book, "Watermelon Pete & Other Stories," small format w/illustrated cover & color illustrations by Elizabeth Gordon, hard cover, 68 pp. ... **100**

Christmas card, postcard size, "The Night Before Christmas - Christmas Greetings," color scene of black mother looking down at her children in bed while holding toys behind her back, art by R.F. Outcault, 1909 (ILLUS., top right).. **95**

Decals, sheet of eight different Golliwoggs in red, yellow, blue, black & white, each 1 1/4" h., the sheet **95**

Two Victorian Die-cuts of a Black Man & Lady

Die-cut, color lithographed paper, bust of fashionable black man smoking & fashionable black woman w/powder puff, some wear, late 19th c., pr. (ILLUS. above).................... **45**

Die-cut of Dancing Black Man

Die-cut, Victorian paper cut-out of dancing black man wearing vest & striped pants & holding cigar, ca. 1890s (ILLUS.)...................................... **45**

Fashion print, "Isabelle - Costumes du XVIIIe Siecle par Doucet," Po-

French Fashion Print

choir-type, possibly from the "Gazette du Bon Ton," 1912-14, in shades of brown, tan & green, 6 1/2 x 7" (ILLUS.)....................... **100-150**

Flyer, "Don't Let Them Burn! - Free the 9 Scottsboro Boys," six-panel paper, published by International Labor Defense, cover photo of protesters, includes petitions to fill out & photos of the defendants, 4 x 9 1/2"... **168**

French Magazine with Baker Cover

Magazine, "A-Z Hebdomadaire Illustré," cover photo of Josephine Baker, France, 1932 (ILLUS.) **85**

Josephine Baker on Ciné-Miroir Cover

Magazine, "Ciné-Miroir," December 14, 1934, French magazine on movie stars, early cover photo of Josephine Baker in fancy costume (ILLUS.).......... **125**

ABC Magazine with Josephine Baker

Magazine, "ABC," June 21, 1958, color cover photo of Josephine Baker & three of her adopted children, Belgium (ILLUS.) **75**

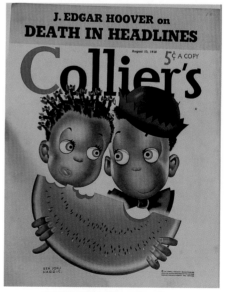

1938 Collier's Magazine Cover

Magazine, "Collier's," August 13, 1938, comic cover cartoon drawing of black girl & boy eating watermelon, artwork by Ben Jorj Harris (ILLUS.) **75-100**

Josephine Baker de Post Cover Photo

Magazine, "de Post," January 22, 1956, large cover photo of Josephine Baker being fitted in a Pierre Balmain gown, w/her husband Joe Bouillon & designer Balmain, Belgium (ILLUS.)...................................... **125**

Josephine Baker Jet Magazine Cover

Magazine, "Jet," July 5, 1973, cover close-up photo of Josephine Baker, cover story "Josephine Baker - Sexty-Seven and Still on the Top," covers her fifty-year career (ILLUS.).......... **50**

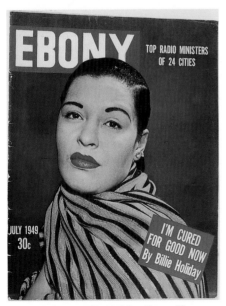

Ebony with Billie Holiday Cover Photo

Magazine, "Ebony," July 1949, color cover photo of Billie Holiday (ILLUS.).... **125**

Jours de France Josephine Baker Issue

Magazine, "Jours de France," April 28 - May 4, 1975, color cover photo of Josephine Baker in costume, covers her death, France (ILLUS.) **100**

1897 Judge Christmas Issue

Magazine, "Judge," special "Xmas Judge," 1897, color cover vignette of black girl wearing red dress & standing under mistletoe, titled "Come Kiss Me Honey," green holly leaves in border, illustrations by Kemble (ILLUS.) **125**

Josephine Baker in Le Soir Illustré

Magazine, "Le Soir Illustré," February 23, 1950, large cover photo of Josephine Baker performing (ILLUS.).......... **75**

Early Josephine Baker La Rampe Cover

Magazine, "La Rampe," early cover photo of Josephine Baker, ca. 1920s or 1930s (ILLUS.)..................... **125**

Le Sourire Josephine Baker 1933 Cover

Magazine, "le Sourire," January 26, 1933, early cover photo of Josephine Baker w/a leopard, cover story titled "Son Troisieme Amour" (Her Third Love, i.e., the leopard) (ILLUS.) **100**

Magazine, "Liberation," December 1956, special issue released during the Montgomery bus boycott, early article by Martin Luther King as well as E.D. Nixon, Eleanor Roosevelt, Ralph Bunche, Roy Wilkins & others, yellow cover w/bus boycott drawing, 20 pp., cover soiling, 8 1/2 x 10 3/4"..................................... **281**

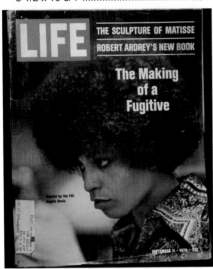

"Life" Magazine Featuring Angela Davis

Magazine, "Life," September 11, 1970 issue, cover photo & story on Angela Davis, covers her life & career, complete in excellent condition (ILLUS.)....... **75**

Magazine, "Noir et Blanc," March 3-9, 1966, large cover photo of a smiling Josephine Baker below a headline translated from French to read "Josephine Baker: She Is Saved!" (ILLUS.)..... **65**

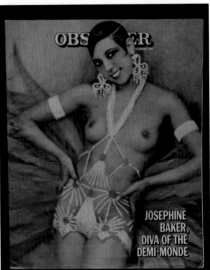

Observer Cover with Josephine Baker

Magazine, "Observer," January 19, 1986, early cover photo of Josephine Baker in risque costume, eight-page feature on her life & career, English (ILLUS.).......................... **90**

Noir et Blanc with Josephine Baker

Paris Match with Josephine Baker

Magazine, "Paris Match," April 26, 1975, color cover photo of Josephine Baker in costume, four-page tribute to her life & career, born June 3, 1906, died in 1975, France (ILLUS. previous page)...................................... **100**

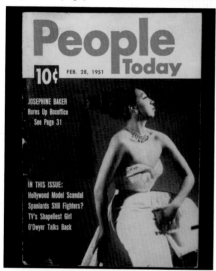

1950s Josephine Baker Magazine Cover

Magazine, "People Today," February 28, 1951, cover photo of Josephine Baker in fancy gown (ILLUS.) **45**

1924 Pictorial Review Cover

Magazine, "Pictorial Review," September 1924, comical color cover picture of black girl holding large slice of watermelon, illustration by Nell Holt (ILLUS.) **75-80**

Point de Vue Josephine Baker Issue

Magazine, "Point de Vue Images du Monde," March 3, 1949, color cover photo of Josephine Baker in costume, inside two-page story on her Revue & some of the costumes she will wear, France (ILLUS.).................... **75**

Josephine Baker Quick Magazine Cover

Magazine, "Quick," August 13, 1951, cover photo of Josephine Baker in fancy gown holding a large fan, magazine for the African-American audience w/an inside story on the struggles of Negro entertainers (ILLUS. previous page) **60**

Magazine, "Quick Pocket News Weekly," October 6, 1952, Jackie Robinson cover photo, report on the 1952 World Series, w/original mailer **25-35**

Josephine Baker Regarde Cover

Magazine, "Regarde," June 13, 1947, cover photo of Josephine Baker w/an elaborate head wrap, France (ILLUS.) **75**

Josephine Baker on Sepia Cover

Magazine, "Sepia," November 1960, publication for the African-American market, features photo of Josephine Baker in feathered costume, cover feature titled "The Fabulous, Ageless Josephine Baker" (ILLUS.) **150**

Magazine, "TV Digest," the week of October 28, 1950, features Ethel Waters, star of "Beulah," Volume 4, No. 43, for the Philadelphia - New Jersey market **45**

Spanish Language Television Guide

Magazine, "Zig Zag TeleGuia," September 27, 1967, television guide in Spanish w/cover picture of The Supremes, Santiago, Chile (ILLUS.)....... **125**

Magazine advertisement, "Gold Dust Washing Powder," printed in black & white, shows the Twins, one holding large mirror while the other stands in front of it, reads across the top "Let the GOLD DUST Twins do your work," an open box of the product shown w/the Twins and further advertising across the bottom, from "Good Housekeeping" magazine, 1908 .... **75**

GOLLIWOGG
A VIGNY ODOR

GOLLIWOGG'S enchanting smile was his letter of introduction—that subtle smile that made the ladies of America wonder what charms he conceals to make him so gay.

And the exquisite fragrance of GOLLIWOGG Perfume de Vigny, Paris—has charmed his acquaintances into most intimate friends.

GOLLIWOGG is the mascot, the idol of ladies everywhere—"demande a Paris!" ask New York! and if you would like to see the "Lucky Little Feller" for yourself, he has an address: Any Store, Any State, America.

Can be had in Toilette Waters and Powders. At all good dealers.

LIONEL TRADING CO., INC.
320 Fifth Avenue   New York

1920s Golliwogg Perfume Magazine Ad

Magazine advertisement, "Golliwogg - A Vigny Odor...," features Golliwogg figural perfume bottle & original box, from "Vanity Fair," 1920s (ILLUS.) **40**

Magazine advertisement, "'KISLAV' - Gant Mat - Garanti Lavable..." glove advertisement in French showing black bellhop holding box of gloves for fashionable young white woman, Pochoir-type, from "Art, Gout & Beauté," 1920s, 6 x 8" (ILLUS. below) **45**

Parfum Jane Hading Magazine Ad

Magazine advertisement, "Parfum Jane Hading aux Roses D'Orient...," black & white perfume ad from French magazine, Pochoir-type, from "Gazette de BonTon," March 1913 (ILLUS.) **40**

Magazine advertisement, "The Gold Dust Twins Paint Box," printed in color, the open box lid showing four rows of different colors, ca. 1928 .... **50**

Magazine advertisement, "Topsy Doll," ad for cloth doll showing the uncut sheet that was available, from "Good Housekeeping," early 20th c. **50**

French Kislav Glove Advertisement

Early Train Ad with Black Porter

Magazine advertisement, "Trains of the Modern World - Edward G. Budd Manufacturing Company. Philadelphia. Detroit," color full-age ad featuring train cars built by Budd & a smiling black train porter, from the "New Yorker," 1950s (ILLUS.) **45**

Dr. King "Time" Cover from a Group

Magazine covers, "Time," group of five each autographed by the subject of the cover picture, includes

Dr. Martin Luther King, Jr. (minor folds & three punch holes along edge), Robert Staubach (minor folds & three punch holes along edge), Barry Goldwater (light signature, minor folds, three punch holes along edge), Hugo L. Black (three punch holes along edge) & Richard Nixon (minor folds, bold signature), dates range from 1963 to 1972, King autograph is scarce, the group (ILLUS. of Dr. King cover) **1,730**

Map, woodcut, map of the Southern slavery states, titled "Moral Map of U.S. - Jan. 1837," proof copy by John Hall, Albany, New York, mounted on album page, 6 x 6" (minor foxing, tear w/paper loss not into image) **154**

Meeting ticket, "Massachusetts Anti-Slavery Society - The Board of Managers will meet on Wednesday Oct. 1st, 1851 at 10 1/2 o'clock a.m. at 21 Cornhill, R.F. Wallcut, Rec. Sec.," card stock, 2 3/8 X 3 1/2" (very slightly browned) **69**

French Cruise Ship Menu

Menu, cruise ship, color cover image of a black woman, issued by the Compagnie des Messageries Maritimes, France, ca. 1950s (ILLUS.)........ **45**

Military order, General Butler's General Order #88, New Orleans, H.Q. of the Gulf, November 1, 1862, reads "No person will be arrested as a slave...unless...owned by a loyal citizen of the United States," disbound, one page **83**

Movie flier, newsprint, "Joe Louis vs Tommy Farr," notes details of the filmed bout including "Why didn't Joe Louis get in that right?," photos of the two boxers, 9 x 12" (some browning) **30-40**

Movie flier, two-sided paper, "Uncle Tom's Cabin - Five Acts," printed in blue & tan, from the World Film Corp., lists & has photos of the various lead characters w/unnamed black man playing Uncle Tom, ca. 1920, 8 1/4 x 10 1/2" (folds, slight browning, some stains) **75**

Movie Poster for "The Negro Sailor"

Movie poster, "All-American Digest Presents - The Negro Sailor," printed in red, black & white, a row of small black & white photo scenes at the right, 1940s, one-sheet, 27 x 41" (ILLUS.) **598**

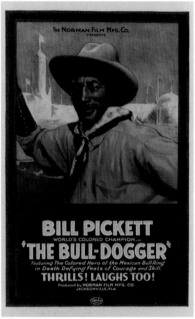

Scarce Bill Pickett Movie Poster

Movie poster, "Bill Pickett - 'The Bull-Dogger,'" Norman Film Mfg. Co., large color image of the cowboy star in the upper section, black & white title section below, 1923, one-sheet, linen-backed, 27 x 41" (ILLUS.).. **3,585**

Movie poster, "Emperor Jones," starring Paul Robeson, color bust portrait of the star, tempera and/or gouache on board, United Artists, 1933, 24 1/2 x 32" .... **3,000+**

Movie poster, "Paradise in Harlem," starring Frank Wilson & Mamie Smith, colored lithograph w/sketched vignettes, black, yellow & red lettering on red background, Jubilee, 1939, one-sheet, linen-backed, 27 x 41".......................... **500-525**

Movie poster, "The Green Eyed Monster," The Norman Film Mfg. Co., 1921, colored lithograph showing a seated black couple, one-sheet, linen-backed, 27 x 41" .... **4,300+**

"The Girl From Chicago" Window Card

Movie window card, "The Girl From Chicago - Oscar Micheaux's All Talking - with Grace Smith - Carl Mahon and an all star Colored Cast," three-quarters length color photo of the star along right side, red box on left side w/yellow & white wording, 1932, 12 x 22" (ILLUS.) **1,076**

Newspaper, "Harper's Weekly," November 24, 1883, cover engraving of Frederick Douglass, his biography included, complete issue (slight browning, margin pin holes from earlier binding)................................... **108**

Pamphlet, paper, "Tract No. 7. One More Appeal to Professors of Religion, Ministries, and Churches, Who Are Not Enlisted in the Struggle Against Slavery," by William Goodell for the New England Anti-Slavery Tract Assoc., ca. 1840s, never bound, 8 pp., 4 1/2 x 7 1/4" (slight soiling) **100**

Melon Family Caricature Playing Cards

CANTALOUPE MELON, The Coachman's Daughter.

WASHINGTON MELON, The Coachman's Son.

Melon Family Caricature Playing Cards

Playing cards, from an early card game, black caricatures on several cards including "Caesar Melon, Dr. Busby's Coachman," "Cantaloupe Melon, The Coachman's Daughter," "Dinah Melon, The Coachman's Wife" & "Washington Melon, The Coachman's Son," set of four (ILLUS. bottom previous page & above) **60**

Postcard, black boy & girl swimming near shore, reads "I Love the Sea When You Are In It!" (ILLUS. right) **30**

Postcard, color comic scene, "A Chip O' The Old Block," art by Bernhardt Wall, Cute Coons Series No. 70, child pulling leg of fleeing hen, Ullman Mfg. Co., No. 1852, 1906 (ILLUS. top of next page) **35**

Postcard, color comic scene, "Darktown Doctors," art by R.F. Outcault, Darktown Series No. 76, scene of black doctors consulting, a frightened patient in the background, Ullman Mfg. Co., No. 1891 (ILLUS. center of next page) **65**

" I LOVE THE SEA WHEN YOU ARE IN IT ! "

Postcard with Two Children Swimming

"A Chip O' The Old Block" Postcard

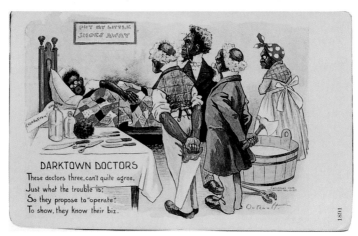

"Darktown Doctors" Postcard

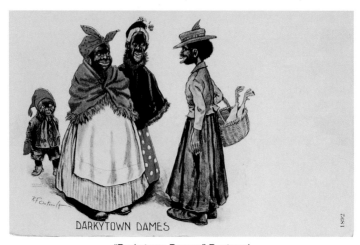

"Darkytown Dames" Postcard

Postcard, color comic scene, "Darky-town Dames," art by R.F. Outcault, Darktown Series No. 76, group of black women gossiping, Ullman Mfg. Co., No. 1892 (ILLUS. bottom, previous page) **65**

Comic Black Boy & Goose Postcard

Postcard, color comic scene, "Deed, I didn't steal um!," art by Bernhardt Wall, Little Coons Series No. 59, black boy holding large goose, Ullman Mfg. Co., No. 1661 (ILLUS.) **25**

Postcard with Cute Black Child

Postcard, color comic scene, "Does yo' want a little honey?," art by C.H. Twelvetrees, cute black child, Edward Gross, No. 7, ca. 1915 (ILLUS.) **30**

Postcard, color comic scene, "He Lubs Me," art by Bernard Wall, Cute Coons Series No. 70, black girl seated pulling petals from sunflower, Ullman Mfg. Co., No. 1854, 1906 (ILLUS. below)...................................... **50**

"He Lubs Me" Comic Postcard

Postcard, color comic scene, "I'se not light-headed - I'se a Brunette," art by C.H. Twelvetrees, Edward Gross, No. 44.. **35**

Comic "Just Two Coons" Postcard

Postcard, color comic scene, "Just Two Coons," art by Bernhardt Wall, Little Coons Series No. 59, black boy w/raccoon, Ullman Mfg. Co., No. 1663 (ILLUS.)................................. **25**

Postcard, color comic scene, "Koontown Kids," art by R.F. Outcault, group of black children w/baby in cart, Darktown Series No. 76, Ullman Mfg. Co., No. 1889 (ILLUS. below)................. **65**

Comic Man & Wife Postcard

Postcard, color comic scene, "Little Dolly Daydreams - the Pride of Idaho," black man pulling corset tight on his wife, postal cancel in 1912 (ILLUS.)........ **40**

Postcard, color comic scene, "Who's dat say chickun?," art by Bernhardt Wall, Little Coons Series No. 59, black boy w/chicken, Ullman Mfg. Co., No. 1662 .... **30**

Postcard, color comic scene, "Whose baby is OO?," art by Bernhardt Wall, Cute Coons Series No. 70, shows a face-off between a black baby & a pig, Ullman Mfg. Co., No. 1853, 1906..... **30**

"Koontown Kids" Postcard by Outcault

WON'T YOU BE MY CHOCOLATE DROP?

Comic Postcard with Black Children

I " YOU ALL CAN HAB DE RINE."

Black Boy with Watermelon Postcard

Postcard, color comic scene, "Won't You Be My Chocolate Drop," black children on a kitchen counter (ILLUS.) **35**

Postcard, color comic scene, "You all can hab de rine," art by Bernhardt Wall, Little Coons Series No. 59, black

boy holding half a watermelon & a doll, Ullman Mfg. Co., No. 1660 (ILLUS.) **25**

Postcard, color, "Just We Two - In Our Little Canoe!," a comical black couple in a small canoe (ILLUS. below)............. **30**

"JUST WE TWO — IN OUR LITTLE CANOE!"

Black Couple in Canoe Postcard

Postcard with Native Couple in Palm

Postcard, color, "Just You and Me - Where No One Can See!," native couple in a palm tree (ILLUS.) **30**

Black Girl in Bed Comic Postcard

Postcard, color, "Look Before You Sleep!," black girl in bed w/black boy coming out from under bed (ILLUS.)...... **40**

Postcard, color, "Memories of Days Gone By - Great Poultry Show," from E.C. Kropp, Milwaukee, No. 385, 1906..... **20**

Postcard, lithographed photo in black & white, titled at bottom "A Colored Baptism," shows four men in river w/someone between them, large crowd on bank, No. 920, undivided back, ca. 1905, unused **35**

Postcard, real photo of entertainer Josephine Baker posed w/real leopard, Piaz Studio, Paris, ca. 1920s **121**

Postcard, real photo-type, black World War I doughboy seated on stool in full dress uniform, studio shot (slightly soiled, lower left corner bend & ding)................................. **80**

Postcard, real photo-type, black World War I doughboy standing w/arms crossed amid barracks, signed "Jack Steger" on the back, also "An AEF photo of yours truly," sold w/original hat shown w/initials in ink inside the flap, 2 pcs. **83**

Postcard, real photo-type, group photo of all-black "Co. D 8th I.N.G. Camp Beng. Harrison Sept. '08," handwritten inscription across bottom front, shown in uniform holding rifles, unused (slightly soiled) **180**

Postcard, real photo-type, group photo of Illinois Infantry colored band in fancy dress uniforms, dated 1908 (postally used, slightly soiled)...... **195-200**

Postcard, real photo-type, hand-tinted, group of black boys along rail fence, captioned "The Mule Race at Coonville, 'Here Comes de Winner,'" marked in lower right corners "Copyright 1896 by F.L. Howe" (ILLUS. top of next page) **100**

Postcard, real photo-type, hand-tinted picture of black child w/bundle of kindling on its head, dated 1907.......... **30**

Postcard, real photo-type, titled on front corner "Tuskegee Students at O'Briens," photograph of black waiters & cooks in training at O'Briens in Waverly, New York, ca. 1930s-40s, was mounted **40**

Postcard, sweet little black boy holding cigarette, captioned "Dis Am Fine" **45**

Real Photo Tinted Postcard of Black Boys

*Partial Set of French Postcards
with a Black Child*

Postcards, set of French cards, each w/black child wearing red cap & standing amid daisies & asking a romantic question shown in French & English below, art by A. Wuyts, early 20th c., set of 6 (ILLUS. of three).. **100+**

Poster, boxing, "Big Boxing Contest - All Star Show - Columbia Theatre - Friday Night, October 8th, 1915 - 9 O'Clock...," listing of black boxers including Willie Langford of New York & center photo of one boxer, also notes "Balcony Reserved for Colored People," 14 x 22" (well worn, folds, slight browning, edge wear & tears, small margin hole). **175-200**

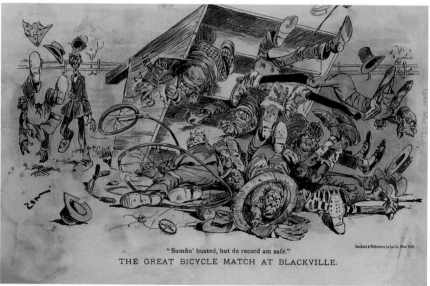

"Sumfin' busted, but de record am safe."
Sackett & Wilhelms Litho Co. New York

THE GREAT BICYCLE MATCH AT BLACKVILLE.

Two Scenes from a Black Comical Bicycle Race Poster

Poster, boxing, color photograph of Muhammad Ali depicted as martyr & saint, standing in his boxing trunks, his body pierced w/drawn-in arrows, produced in response to Ali's draft resistance & his being stripped of his heavyweight boxing crown, ca. 1969, 20 x 25" (fold at top edge).. **40-50**

Poster, comical, heavy cardboard, series of full-color comic scenes titled "The Great Bicycle Match at Blackville," each scene captioned, w/a fold-out back support for display, Sackett & Wilhelms Litho. Co., New York, late 19th - early 20th c., 11 1/2 x 14", complete poster (ILLUS. of two scenes above) .... **125+**

Rare Josephine Baker 1930s Poster

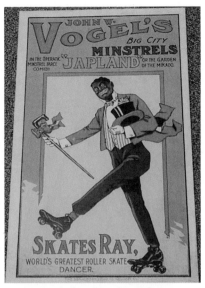

Vogel's Minstrels Show Poster

Color Poster for Minstrel Songs

Poster, "Josephine Baker," large stylized Art Deco bust portrait of Baker by Jean Chassaing, Paris, 1931, large size, rare (ILLUS.)................ **16,100**

Poster, lithographed paper, "George Thatcher's Minstrels - The Darktown Brotherhood vs. the Blackville League," a colorful comic baseball scene w/black players in action, in walnut shadowbox frame, late 19th c., 29 x 39 1/2" **4,950**

Poster, miniature, paper, oval vignetted photo of young black couple above advertising for "The Celebrated Armstrongs - America's Greatest Colored Magicians," 1911 tour, about 4 3/4 x 7" (edges appear trimmed, some light creased) **200**

Poster, minstrel show, "John W. Vogel's Big City Minstrels - 'Japland' - Skates Ray - World's Greatest Roller Skate Dancer," colorful image of man in blackface roller skating, in red, blue, black & cream, early 20th c., creasing, light soiling, 12 x 20" (ILLUS. above right)............................ **106**

Poster, "Minstrel Songs and Negro Melodies from the Sunny South," color scene of young black man standing at left wearing work clothes, a cotton field in the background, a listing of song sheets for sale in a long box at right side, late 19th - early 20th c. (ILLUS.) **311**

Extremely Rare 1929 Moulin Rouge Poster

Poster, "Moulin Rouge - La Revue Black Birds," large stylized images of two black men flanking a stylish black woman, artwork by Paul Colin, Paris, 1929, large, extremely rare (ILLUS.).............................. **167,500**

Very Rare French "Bal Negre" Poster

Poster, "Théatre des Champs Élysées - le 11 Février 1927 à 23 heurs - Bal Nègre," large stylized figures of black man dancing w/Josephine Baker-style woman, artwork by Paul Colin, Paris, 1927, large, very rare (ILLUS. above) **96,000**

Press kit, for the English movie "The Tunnel," starring Paul Robeson, Supreme Productions, story of Welsh coal mining w/scene of miners on the sepia & pink cover, a Michael Balcon Production, includes press blurbs, five posters & advertising on the back, ca. late 1930s, 11 x 17" (slight soiling, edge & fold wear) **200**

Print, color portrait of Josephine Baker in her famous banana skirt, early 20th c. (ILLUS. top left, next page)....... **25**

Color Print of Josephine Baker

Another Josephine Baker Color Print

Print, color portrait of Josephine Baker in her famous banana skirt, early 20th c. (ILLUS. bottom left) **25**

Print, color scene of ballroom w/stylized sketched black men & white women, art by Chas. La Borde, France, 1912 .... **150+**

Print, "Eighth Illinois Regiment Now in France," black & white photolithograph, World War I era, gives brief history of the unit since the Spanish-American War, notes "over 157,000 Negro troops either in France or on their way," two views of the troops in rank outside large public building, E. Renesch, Chicago, 11 1/2 x 15 1/2" (slight cover crease, two small edge tears).. **125-150**

"Sambo's Baby's Christening" Print

Print, "Sambo's Baby's Christening," part of comic series illustrating African American life in late Victorian America, by John Delve Ilfracomre, ca. 1916 (ILLUS.) **225**

Print, "Sambo's Courtship," part of comic series illustrating African American life in late Victorian America, by John Delve Ilfracomre, ca. 1916 (ILLUS. top of next page) **225**

"Sambo's Courtship" Comic Print

"Sambo's Twins" Comic Print

Print, "Sambo's Twins," part of comic series illustrating African American life in late Victorian America, by John Delve Ilfracomre, ca. 1916 (ILLUS.) **225**

"Sambo's First Born" Comic Print

Print, "Sambo's First Born," part of comic series illustrating African American life in late Victorian America, by John Delve Ilfracomre, ca. 1916 (ILLUS.) **225**

"Sambo's Wedding" Comic Print

Print, "Sambo's Wedding," part of comic series illustrating African American life in late Victorian America, by John Delve Ilfracomre, ca. 1916 (ILLUS.) **225**

Josephine Baker "Bambino" Program

Program, for "Bambino," features photo of Josephine Baker in costume, 66-page booklet for her last live performance in 1975, very rare (ILLUS.) ... **250**

Josephine Baker 1964 Playbill Cover

Program, "Playbill - Josephine Baker and Her Company," February 1964, at the Brooks Atkinson Theatre, New York City, cover photo of Josephine Baker in costume (ILLUS.) **50**

Program, "The Negro and the Flag - At the Nation's Service," Lincoln Day Program, sponsored by the Freedmen's Aid Society of the Methodist Episcopal Church, honors black World War I veterans w/fundraising appeal, red & blue cover, 12 pages, 6 x 9" (slightly soiled, price tag pull) .... **75+**

Program with autograph, "American Negro Exposition - 1863 - 1940 - Chicago Coliseum - July 4 to Sept. 2 - Official Program and Guide Book," colorful cover art of black couple in foreground w/shadow of Lincoln's head behind, includes many photos w/autograph of Joe Louis over photo of someone else, celebrates 75 years of Emancipation, 64 pp... **754**

Early Pillsbury Color Advertisement

Sign, cardboard, "Pillsbury's Best," color scene of two black children sailing in round wooden tub, advertising on the waving pennant & sail, wording in the waves reads "Pillsbury's Best is the Best," late 19th - early 20th c., 8 1/2 x 11" (ILLUS.) .... **250+**

O'Baby Chocolate Dairy Drink Sign

Sign, "O'Baby Chocolate Dairy Drink," lithographed cardboard, caricature of black boy holding bottle of the product, reads "O'Baby - Chocolate Dairy Drink - Pure - Wholesome - Tasty - 'Ain't dat sumptin' - It's pasteurized - No Preservatives," printed in brown, green, orange, white & black, paint loss quarter of way up at bottom, edge wear, 14 1/4 x 22 1/2" (ILLUS.) **300**

Bus Segregation Sign

Sign, segregation-type, "Negroes Must Move To The Back of The Bus - Sparta, Miss. Transit," ca. 1950s, 11 1/2 x 14 1/2" (ILLUS.) **200**

Two Rest Rooms Segregation Signs

Signs, segregation-type, for rest rooms, framed paper, black & white printing, each (ILLUS. of two) **60**

Signs, segregation-type, painted metal, wood or paper, types such as "Colored," "White" or "Colored Must Sit In Balcony," depending on size, material, wording & condition, each **500-1,000**

Slavery document, estate inventory in Virginia, includes five slaves, names slave men & women & their relative values, estate of Thomas Douglas, dated January 5, 1802, court document w/embossed 50¢ revenue stamp, 4 pages, 7 x 12"........ **150**

Slavery document, runaway slave court document, dated Prince George's Co., Maryland, 11/23/1850, reads in part "Negro woman Maria and her child Paul...the proper slaves of one William N. Dorsett...with force and arms...on the thirtieth day of November (1847) did then and there unlawfully and wickedly escape and runaway..." they escaped to Washington, D.C. but were apprehended three years later & the owner now seeks their return, hand-written, w/seal blindstamped, 7 x 12" **280-300**

Slavery document, slave bill of sale, court document, notes "A woman slave aged about twenty years and called Margaret...for the sum of Eight Hundred and Fifty Dollars," sold to Joseph Johnston, on blue paper, Tennessee, 1854, folds, 8 x 9 1/2" **250-275**

Slavery document, slave bill of sale, hand-written, noted "Negro Wench, Named Peg, about Twenty years of Age," sold for 55 pounds "Current Money of the Province of New York," at Newtown, Queens County, New York, 1779, w/original seals, 8 x 10 1/2" (slight browning, some separation at folds) **1,000-1,200**

Slavery document, slave bill of sale, hand-written, notes George F. Barnes sold Negro Girl Francis, aged about 15 to Thomas Huntby (illeg.), 2 June, 1845 for $350, St. Louis, Missouri, 7 1/2 x 10" (folds, small dark spots) **250**

Slavery document, slave bill of sale, hand-written, Pleasant P. Wilson (Andrew Co.) sold Slave Lewis to G.B. Thorp (Holt Co.), Lewis was aged 12 & sold for $300, dated October 23, 1852, in Missouri, on blue-lined paper, 7 x 9" (browned & chipped edges, old crumpling along left margin) **200**

Slavery document, slaves hired on a ship, 1830, Orange Gaylord hired from John Vandown for $12/mo. "negro boys Nat & Spencer for firemen on M.S. Liberty," 8 1/2" sq. (folds, few small brown spots) **160**

Slavery document, states that "Mr. Capps buys Negro of Joseph Bates for $679.00, Dec. 14, 1846," written in blue & brown ink, found near Mobile, Alabama, 7 1/2 x 12 1/4" (fold lines & a few pinpoint holes) .... **250+**

Song sheet, hand-written lyrics to Emancipation song "The Contraband of Port Royal," on Chicago and NorthWestern Railway Co. note paper, several stanzas included, Chicago, ca. 1863 .... **125**

Songsheet-broadside, "The Sorrows of Yamba - Or - The Negro Woman's Lamentation," published by Cheap Repository, England, w/woodcut of slave woman & white man on tropical dockside, ca. 1795, 10 3/4 x 17" **1,265**

Spot Removal Information Wheel

Spot removal information wheel, die-cut paper figural of a stylized smiling Mammy holding open a large book, a hole in the page shows a round wheel printed w/tips on how to remove spots, ca. 1940s (ILLUS.) **125**

Subscription receipt, paper, for "The Liberator," William Lloyd Garrison's abolitionist newspaper, signed by publisher Henry W. Williams, 1841, 3 x 7 1/2" (couple of minor tears) **150**

Paul Robeson "Othello" Poster

Black Cupid with Watermelon & Chickens Valentine

Theatre window card, "Othello" starring Paul Robeson, Theatre Guilde presentation at the Shubert Theatre, large image of Robeson in costume standing against golden brown background, minor staining & imperfections in the white border, 14 x 22" (ILLUS. bottom of previous page).. **549**

Ticket, "1854-55 - Anti-Slavery Bazaar - 15 Winter Street - Season - No Transfer," card stock, slightly browned edge, 2 x 3 1/8".................... **220**

Valentine, comic, postcard-type, a black Cupid being attacked by chickens in front of large watermelon, reads "To my Valentine - De troubles ob true lub ain't a few - But nothin' can't keep mah lub from you," Raphael Tuck & Sons, Ltd., England, 1906 (ILLUS. top of page) **40-50**

Valentine, comic, postcard-type, black boy in sailor suit standing between Teddy bear & small dog, art by R.F. Outcault, long verse reads "I dreams erbout yo' every night - I thinks of yo' by Day - I spec's yo' is my Valentine - it cert'ny looks dat way," copyright 1903 by Raphael Tuck (postal cancel over figure, pencil writing on front).................... **30-40**

Comic Valentine with Chubby Black Girl

Valentine, comic, postcard-type, chubby black girl standing pouting, art by C.H. Twelvetrees, verse reads "Ah suttan party am gonna receive flowers but aint gonna smell 'um," 4 x 6" (ILLUS.)............................ **40**

Valentine, comic, postcard-type, long verse w/"Chocolate Cullah Cupid," artwork by R.F. Outcault, early 20th c. (ILLUS. top of next page) **30-40**

Valentine, comic, postcard-type, shows black boy begging on hands & knees for love, reads "Honey, jus a lil bit won't yu?"............................ **30-40**

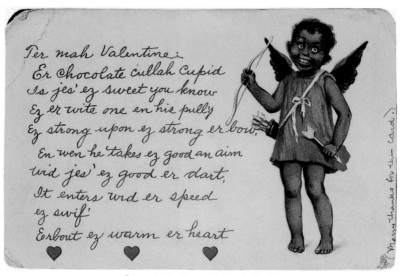

Comic Valentine with Black Cupid

Valentine, die-cut w/moveable mouth, grotesque caricature of walking black man wearing derby & carrying cane & heart w/"To my Valentine," early 20th c. **125**

Valentine, folded comic-type, opens to show two halves of green & red watermelon w/head of black woman in one & black man in the other, each half w/inscription along bottom border, ca. 1918 (ILLUS. below) **150**

Valentine, mechanical, black boy in two-wheeled goat cart wearing large tam & holding card w/heart on it, his head moves as you turn a wheel disk behind the cart wheel, bright colors, 1929 (goat's hoof a bit soft) **125**

Comic Watermelon Couple Valentine

Girl on Stove Comic Valentine

Valentine, mechanical, black girl seated on black cook stove & jointed at waist, dark red background, wording in black across bottom reads "Valentine Greetings - Here's One Hot Mamma Who Could Certainly Warm Up To You," ca. 1930 (ILLUS.)............ **100**

— Chapter 10 —
PHOTOGRAPHIC ITEMS

Ambrotype, African-American gentleman, sixth-plate size, young bearded man seated w/hands clasped & one elbow resting on table, some milky tarnish on edge, in half case, mid-19th c. **$181**

Ambrotype, half-length portrait of young black man w/serious expression sitting holding a closed book in his lap, image mailed to Columbia, South Carolina, during the Civil War but not delivered, in full case w/velvet surface, image w/stain halo around edges & some spots .... **440+**

Cabinet photo, black couple, middle-aged man & wife posed w/the man seated while his full-figured wife stands to his right resting one arm on his shoulder, studio shot by Philadelphia Art Co., Brooklyn, New York, buff mount, gilt edge (slight scuffs) **50**

Cabinet photo, full-length portrait of grinning black man wearing work clothes & seated on rustic branch bench, by Batcham, Norwalk, Ohio, inscribed in ink on the back w/the name of the sitter (slightly soiled) **50**

Cabinet photo, full-length studio portrait of standing black train conductor in uniform, by Norrell, Bloomington, Indiana (very slight foxing & browning) .... **150+**

Cabinet photo, three-quarters length portrait of standing young black Alabama minister Rev. A.J. Rodgers, pastor of the Old Ship Church, by H.P. Tresslar, Montgomery, Alabama, 1894 (some soil, slight foxing) **100+**

Carte de visite, Black Chapel, Richmond, Virginia, written on the back "Mount Calvary Chapel of S. Mary the Virgin (for colored people). Calbraith P. Perry, Priest in Charge" (in ink), "Richmond VA, 1863" in pencil, probably ca. 1875 (some soil, a bit light) **100**

Carte de visite, black Mammy & white child, fine image of cute baby being held by sad-faced black woman, image by Gutekunst w/tax stamp, ca. 1864, Philadelphia (slight stain along bottom edge) .... **240+**

Carte de visite, Charleston, South Carolina, black church interior w/service in progress, pastor pointing toward picture of Christ on the cross & altar, at least eight men & women kneeling at the rail, others seated on benches, by Osborn's Gallery, Charleston, early 1860s-style mount w/gold border (light, a bit foxed, mount & print soil) .... **1,325+**

Carte de visite, elderly black woman, seated wearing a striped dress, slightly crooked smile, by Hagadorn of Poughkeepsie, New York, ca. 1870s.. **60**

Carte de visite, field labor scene, black man, woman & children working picking cotton in field, basket shown, square creamy white mount, ca. 1860s............................... **100**

Carte de visite, Frederick Douglass, shown as late middle-aged man, seated position, ivory mount, written in ink across the bottom edge "Fred Douglas [sic]," slightly vignetted & soiled, probably late 1860s......... **925-950**

Carte de visite, portrait of Sojourner Truth, famous guide on the Underground Railroad, printed under the image "I Sell the Shadow to Support the Substance," copyrighted by her on the base, 1864......................... **1,575+**

Carte de visite, Private Gordon, young black man sitting shirtless w/his back to the camera to show his whipping wounds, an escaped slave who enlisted in the Union Army in Louisiana in 1863, he had been whipped Christmas Day 1862, served as a Union guide & was recaptured by the Rebels & later found beaten by the U.S. Army & recovered, photograph by Baton Rouge photographers McPherson & Olivier, illustrated in "Men of Color," this copy, titled "The Scourged Back," was published by McAllister & Bros., Philadelphia, written in ink along the bottom edge "Uncle Tom" (soil, foxing, pinhole at top) .... **5,500+**

Carte de visite, young black man seated next to table w/books & small vase of flowers, remnants of tax stamp, 1860s **60**

Carte de visite, young handsome black man seated showing three-quarters view, one arm resting on ornately carved studio table, a fancy urn behind him, copyright by G.W. Barnes, Rockford, Illinois **50**

Daguerreotype, half-length portrait of young black woman w/book, 1/6th plate size, serious expression, her tie & cuffs tinted blue, image some-what faint, rubbed & cleaned, in full case w/repaired spine .... **575+**

Daguerreotype, young black woman, 1/6th plate size, girl in long-sleeved dress & center-parted hair sitting at table, one arm resting on table, brass mat, re-sealed in full case, possibly 1840s **1,000**

Large format photo, dentist's office w/dentist standing & viewing the camera, a patient in the chair turned away from the camera, marked in pencil "Dr. Wallace in Muskogee, Okla," ca. 1920s, 5 x 7" **100**

Large format photo, group shot of black baseball team, black & white, shows sixteen men & four women, ten men in various stages of uni-form, shown at ball field w/equip-ment, probably the Lynchburg, Vir-ginia, White Sox, 7 1/2 x 9 1/2" (pencil writing in sky, stains, soil) **500**

Large format photo, on board, scene of pall bearers in an interior holding minister's casket aloft, unidentified location, names written across bot-tom edge including "Rev. Jones Fu-neral," 4 1/2 x 7" (some scuffing & spots on the mount) **55**

Large format photo, set-back cen-tered image of heavy-set seated black woman in working clothes peel-ing potatoes gazing off to right, grey mount, dark tones, 7 1/4 x 9 1/2" (mount badly broken, image crazed, chipped around edges).......................... **65**

Large format photo, signed on photo "Detachment No. 3, Medical De-partment, Des Moines, Ia," black & white photo on grey mount, group of seated World War I black medical personnel, 1st Lt. J.L. Leach, M.R.C. Commander, each man identified on back, 5 x 7" (some soil, slightly loose mount)........................ **180+**

Large format photo, young black child seated on rug beside stuffed small Boston terrier, fancy studio mount, 5 x 7" **40**

ZEPHYERRE HELIOTROPE WATSON

Magazine Photo of Black Actress

Magazine photograph, copy of a photograph of black stage actress Zephyerre Heliotrope Watson, from Theatre magazine, 1918, the page (ILLUS.).. **25**

Black Lecturer Magic Lantern Slide

Magic lantern slide, black lecturer, single lever mechanical-type, wood mounted, h.p. image of black man at lecture table facing black audi-ence, lever moves lecturer's body, second half 19th c., 4 x 7" (ILLUS.)...... **85**

Photo of Josephine Baker in Gown

Hattie McDaniel Signed Photograph

Photograph, black & white image of Josephine Baker wearing a Pierre Balmain evening gown, 1956 (ILLUS.).......... **75**

Photograph, black & white portrait of actress Hattie McDaniel shown wearing long mink coat & standing by fireplace of her Beverly Hills home, personally inscribed & dated 1944, minor border tear (ILLUS. top right)... **759**

Photograph, black & white silver gelatin print, titled "Dixie Belles," portrait of two pretty seated young African-American women wearing straw hats & light-colored dresses, shot by Theodore "Fonville" Winans (Louisiana, 1911-1992), signed & dated 1938, 16 x 20" (ILLUS. below)................................ **5,520**

Winans Photo of "Dixie Belles"

Photograph, Cab Calloway, signed 8 x 10" professional glossy black & white photo, shows Calloway & his Cotton Club Orchestra, inscribed "To Mike - Sorry I didn't see you this trip. Lots of Luck. Hi-di Ho, Cab Calloway," bold clear signature (minor bends, writing on back) **75**

Rare Photo of Josephine Baker

Photograph, entertainer Josephine Baker in her famous "banana" costume worn at the Follies Bergere in Paris, sepia tone, 1920s, rare original print (ILLUS.) .... **200+**

Real photo postcard, portrait of S. Helen Porter, teacher at Tuskegee Institute, shown seated at her desk, ca. 1910, inscribed on back "To my dear Cora with every good wish of S. Helen Porter" (slightly soiled, paper clip rust in upper right) **55**

Real photo postcard, standing older black woman dressed in black facing left & looking at her three daughters, two standing & one seated, all dressed in white, ca. 1910, not postally used but signed on back "Martha Henderson, 306 Climan St. Cheboygan, MI" on back (lower left corner dinged) **45**

Stereoview, arched double image of young male banjo player seated wearing cap & striped outfit, strip label w/"music on the brain," square cream mount, late 1860s **125**

Stereoview, double image of full-length standing elderly black man dressed in rags & holding bundle & stick, by Land, a chemist in Columbus, Georgia, ca. 1860s (a few tiny spots) ... **150**

Stereoview, double view of young black chimney sweeps w/brushes & scrapers, wearing sloppy clothes & hats, may be from a negative by J.N. Wilson, Savannah, Georgia, titled "Picturesque Views of All Countries," yellow rounded cream mount (upper right corner worn, lower corner slightly bent) **100**

"Uncle Isaac Selling Wood" Stereo View

Stereoview, occupational, "Uncle Isaac Selling Wood," J.A. Palmer, Aiken, South Carolina, #137, second half 19th c. (ILLUS.) **95**

Stereoview, ox cart scene w/black man riding ox puling small cart, titled "15th Amendment bringing his crop to town," by J.N. Wilson, Savannah, Georgia, No. 126, ca. 1871, probably meant to ridicule newly enfranchised black voters, yellow mount **150**

Stereoview, titled "Cabin Home, Petersburg, Va," shows black figures outside crude cabin, Kilburn No. 885, yellow ground & rounded corner mount (minor edge wear, slight mount soiling) **70**

Stereoview, titled "Jack and Abby Landlord, aged 100 and 110 years," shows two ex-slaves seated side by side in studio setting & wearing rough clothes, he holding an upright rifle, No. 79, J.N. Wilson, Savannah, Georgia, ca. 1875 (mounting soil, cracked tack holes) **125**

Stereoview, titled "The famous 10th Colored Cavalry - that climbed San Juan," marching lines of soldiers at the Peace Jubilee, Philadelphia, by Jarvis, 1899, published by Underwood **150-200**

Stereoview, titled "The Little Cabin Home," double exterior view of elderly black man leaning on chimney of rough plant & thatch cabin, Engle & Furlong, Fernandina, Florida, No. 14, Views in Georgia & Florida, rounded ream mount, ca. 1870s (left corners cut) **40**

Tintype, 1/4th plate size, thermoplastic case w/molded scene of Gypsy Fortune Teller, the image showing middle-aged gently smiling Mammy holding small white baby (slight brown stains along lower & left areas of image, case surfaces worn) .. **520+**

Tintype, 1/6th plate size, half-length portrait of pretty black young woman standing wearing hat, gloves, coat w/capelet, third quarter 19th c..... **100**

Tintype, 1/6th plate size, portrait of standing black man, titled "Russell - escaped on Underground Railroad," shows man leaning against pillar holding horseshoe, a hat on the pillar marked "Express," possibly Ohio, ca. 1860 (slight dirt on plate) .. **800+**

Tintype, album-size, comic scene of two black men in studio setting, one pouring from jug into mug while other man holds another cup (streaks at left, minor scratches & bends)...... **180+**

Tintype, full-length studio portrait of imposing middle-aged black woman standing holding closed parasol by her side, her other hand resting beside her fine hat atop an ornate studio chair, ca. 1880, 2 1/2 x 3 1/2" **60**

Tintype, small view of young black girl in full dress, mounted in white embossed paper mount w/oval opening, ca. 1870s, 1 1/4 x 1 1/3" (soiled mounting)................................. **60**

Tintype, young African-American boy, ninth-plate size, charming pose of young boy seated atop draped stool, excellent condition, mid-19th c.. **100**

Tintype, young black woman seated looking to the side, one arm resting on upholstered chair arm, wearing pretty dress w/ruffled sleeves, third quarter 19th c. (scuffed along slight bend above head) **100**

— Chapter 11 —

POLITICAL MEMORABILIA

Advertising photo, "Black is also a Consciousness," Afro-Hair, young boy shown, 1965-1970 .... **$100+**

Badge, "Special Police D.C. - 27 - 29 - August - 1963," celluloid, special March on Washington name tag, pin torn off celluloid on reverse, 2 x 3" .... **100+**

Booklet, "Behind the Florida Bombings - Who Killed NAACP Leader Harry T. Moore and his Wife?," by Joseph North, former editor of New Masses, story of 1952 Klan assassination w/looming figure of Klansman on cover, 23 pages, 5 x 7 1/2". **110+**

Booklet, "Can the States Stop Lynchings?," paper, part of the NAACP anti-lynching campaign, two gruesome photos & documentary evidence of all known lynchings in 1935-36, February 1937, 19 pages, 5 x 7" (cover corners bent, slightly browned) .... **100+**

Booklet, "Equality, Land and Freedom: A Program for Negro Liberation," by the League of Struggle for Negro Rights, large drawn image of black man tearing apart chains, red wraps, November 1933, 48 pages, 4 1/2 x 6" **90**

Booklet, "The Freedom Riders," paper, accounts of participants & different views, published by CORE, 1961, 12 pages, 6 x 8 1/2" **45**

Booklet, "The Position of Negro Women," by Eugene Gordeon & Cyril Briggs, cover photo of young black woman wearing cap, a Communist publication, February 1935, 16 pages, 4 1/2 x 6" **50**

Booklet, "The Republican Party and the Negro - Facts for Party Speakers and Workers," paper, 1952 Republican Congressional Committee, attacks the Democratic record on various issues, 30 pages, 6 x 8 1/4" (slight cover soil & edge wear) **50**

Booklet, "The Story of the Trenton Six," by Elwood Dean, paper, reports the case of six young black men convicted of murder on the basis of "confessions" after prolonged police beatings, 23 pages, December 1949, 5 x 7 1/2" **50**

Booklet, "They Shall Not Die! - Stop The Legal Lynching! - The Story of Scottsboro in Pictures," paper, cover drawing of two black men chopping down large tree marked "Lynching," produced by the League of Struggle for Negro Rights, drawings by A. Refregier, published in March 1932, 16 pages, 5 x 7 1/2" **80**

Brochure, "CORE Interracial Training Institute - Nonviolence in Theory and in Action," paper w/dark mustard yellow ink, dated "Aug. 14 - Sept. 5, 1960, Miami," opens to 8 1/2 x 13 1/2" **50**

Brochure, "CORE Rules for Action," trifold grey paper w/orange ink, image of Ghandi & 13 rules listed for nonviolent action **45**

Flier, "CORE Acts on Voting," paper, folded, brown ink, photos of planning meetings & training in South Carolina, 1958, folded 7 1/2 x 8 1/4" **40**

Flier, "Freedom Ride," paper, promotes documentary movie of that title, printed in red, white & blue, 8 1/2 x 11" (tiny spot, corner bend) **30**

Movie poster, "Freedom Ride," paper, printed in red, white & blue, premiere showing at the University of Rochester, produced by CORE to document journey through the South, hand-written correction in red, 11 x 17" .... **70+**

Pamphlet, "Behind the Lynching of Emmet Louis Till - by Louis Burnham," paper, sketched bust portrait of Till, lynched in Mississippi in 1955, on the cover, 15 pages, 5 x 7 1/4" **50**

Pamphlet, "Lynching & Debt Slavery," paper, by William Pickens, member of the ACLU & early NAACP leader, 1921, 8 pages, 6 x 9" (slightly soiled, foxed, rust stains at staples, spine partially split)............................. **50**

Pamphlet, political, "Remember Your Real Friends - What Has Wendell L. Willkie To Say To the Colored People of America," paper, photo of Willkie w/three black people on the cover, printed in blue ink, for the 1940 presidential campaign, 4 pages, 3 3/4 x 6 1/2" 60

Photo-poster, "Dick Gregory for President," 1968 .... **75-100**

Photo-poster, Huey Newton, Black Panther Party **75-100**

Photograph, Roy Wilkins, black & white glossy print of the Civil Rights leader speaking at the 1963 March on Washington, photo by Cecil Layne, 7 x 10" (wear, ding in lower margin).. 50

Pinback button, "47th Grand Session of Tabor - Jackson, Mississippi - 1889 - 1936 - Mississippi," celluloid sepia & white, wording above two round bust portraits of early leaders, "Rev. Moses Dickson (1846-1901), founder" & "Sir R.E. Smith (1893-1909), pioneer," below the portraits "Fathers of Tabor - Nov. 10-13, 1936," from an early fraternal order, 1 3/4" d. (a few bumps)........................ 35

Pinback button, "All Power To The People," celluloid, black & white, wording at top arching above a photograph of an armed Huey Newton, 1 3/4" d.. 40

Pinback button, "All Power To The People," celluloid, black, yellow & red, wording around border w/sketched bust portrait of Malcolm X in the center, 1 3/4" d. 45

Pinback button, "All Power To The People," celluloid, orange & black, Black Panthers slogan pin w/a leaping black panther in the center & wording in the outer rim band, 1 5/8" d.. 40

Pinback button, "American Negro Labor Congress - 1925," lithographed in purple, white & green, organization lasted only a few months, 7/8" d. 300

Pinback button, "ANGELA DAVIS DAY - Free Angela - Bail Now - Central Park - September 25, 1971," celluloid, neon pink & black, wording above & below bust photograph of Angela Davis, 2" d. .... **50+**

Pinback button, "Black Panther Party - Black Power," celluloid, black & white w/sketched bust portrait of Malcolm X in center, 1 3/4" d. 60

Pinback button, "Black Panther Party - For Self Defense," celluloid, orange & black, silhouetted half-length portrait of Black Panther w/rifle, wording around the border, 1 3/8" d.. 50

Pinback button, "Black Panther Party - Seize The Time," celluloid, neon pink & black, raised black fist holding rifle in center, wording around the border, 1 3/8" d. (slightly scratched).. 50

Pinback button, "Black Panthers," lithographed metal, black & white, Black Panthers raised fist salute in the center, black rim bands, 3 3/8" d. (few very minor rim rubs) 50

Pinback button, "Black Veterans Unite," lithographed metal, black & white, wording above photograph of group of black Vietnam War veterans, ca. 1970, 2 1/4" d. 45

Pinback button, celluloid, design of black & white hands together holding aloft white dove of Peace against blue ground, 1 5/8" d. 20

Pinback button, celluloid, printed black on white bust portrait of Eldridge Cleaver, Black Panther leader, no wording, 1 3/4" d. 25

Pinback button, celluloid w/photo of Bishop W.S. Brooks, 1865-1934, memorial-type, 1 1/4" d. 66

Pinback button, celluloid, white printed equal sign on a black ground, no wording, 5/8" d. 15

Pinback button, "Emancipation March - August 28, 1963 On Washington," black & white celluloid, 1 3/4" d. 83

Pinback button, "free all political prisoners," celluloid, black & orange, a black panther behind bars, wording to the right side, 1 3/8" d. **25**

Pinback button, "Free All Political Prisoners," celluloid, neon pink & black, wording above a half-length caricature of a pig-faced white judge, 1 3/4" d. **20**

Pinback button, "Free Angela," celluloid, orange & black, wording above bust photograph of Angela Davis, 1 1/2" d. **50**

Pinback button, "FREE ANGELA - Free All Political Prisoners," celluloid, orange & black, bust photograph of Angela Davis on the left, wording down the right side, 1 3/4" d. **60**

Pinback button, "Free The N.Y. Panther 21," celluloid, blue & white, blue lettering on a white ground, 1 3/4" d. **20**

Pinback button, "Free The Panther 21," celluloid, yellow w/thin blue stripes, wording above small image of leaping panther, 1 3/4" d. **25**

Pinback button, "Freedom Now," celluloid, torch & wreath in center, white, orange & blue, 2" d. **20**

Pinback button, "Freedom Now," celluloid, torch & wreath in center, white, orange & blue, 7/8" d. **25**

Pinback button, "Freedom Now - CORE" celluloid, upper half w/white lettering on black ground, lower half black lettering on white, from the Congress of Racial Equality, 1 1/2" d. **35**

Pinback button, "Freedom Ride - CORE," celluloid, blue & white, 1961, effort to desegregate interstate buses which provoked violence & a national political crisis, 1 1/2" d. **40**

Pinback button, "I Am For Columbus Negro High School - Are You?," celluloid, blue & white, probably Columbus, Georgia, ca. 1900, 1 1/2" d. .... **60+**

Pinback button, "Labor Says Free Angela TUAD," celluloid, yellow & black from Trade Unionists for Angela Davis, 1" d. (several tiny spots) **30**

Pinback button, "March for Democratic Schools - May 18 - CORE - NAACP," celluloid, black & white, 1 1/4" d. (very slight stain) **40**

Pinback button, "March on Washington for Jobs & Freedom - August 28, 1963," celluloid, black & white w/black & white shaking hands in the center, 2 1/8" d. (bump over pin joint, very small scratches) **100**

Pinback button, "Martin Luther King - For President," bust photo of Dr. King in the center, from 1968 draft-King movement, black & white, by A.G. Trimble, Pittsburgh, 1" d. .... **100+**

Pinback button, "Maryland State Colored Teachers Association - 1937," celluloid, red & white, 5/8" d. **125-150**

Pinback button, "Member - NAACP - 1953," lithographed metal in blue & white, 7/8" d. **55**

Pinback button, "Member - NAACP - 1963," lithographed metal in blue w/white lettering, 1951, 7/8" d. **45**

Pinback button, memorial-type, celluloid, Dr. Martin Luther King, Jr., a picture of Dr. King in center framed by two outer bands, outer one reads "Nonviolence - 'Precious Lord, Take My Hand,'" inner band reads "Dr. Martin Luther King, Jr. - 1929 - 1968," red, white & blue, 3" d. **100**

Pinback button, "NAACP," lithographed metal in blue w/white lettering, 1951, 7/8" d. **50**

Pinback button, "One Man - One Vote - FDP," celluloid, black & white, from the Mississippi Freedom Democratic Party, 1964, 1 1/2" d. **45**

Pinback button, "One Man - One Vote - SNCC," celluloid, from the early 1960s voter registration drives, black & white, 1 1/2" d. **40**

Pinback button, "Poor People's Campaign - 1968," celluloid, stylized portrait of mother & child, black & white, 1" d...... **50**

Pinback button, "Poor People's Campaign - For Poor Power - Rev. Dr. Martin Luther King, Jr.," celluloid, black, white & blue, 3 1/2" d...... **75**

Pinback button, "San Quentin Six," celluloid, yellow & black, wording above six shackled raised fists, 1 3/8" d...... **40**

Pinback button, "Semi-Centennial Celebration of the Battle of Osawatomie & John Brown," celluloid, multicolored w/landscape view of small oval black & white vignette bust of Brown at the bottom edge, lettering in red, dated "Aug. 30 1856-1906," 1 1/2" d. (tiny foxing spots, slight surface wear) ...... **150+**

Pinback button, "SNCC," celluloid, black & white hands shaking above letters, 7/8" d...... **40**

Pinback button, "Soledad Brothers," celluloid, neon pink & black, wording in center framed by a broken chain border, 1 3/8" d...... **25**

Pinback button, "Stop Racist Frame-Up - Free Billy Smith," celluloid, black & white, wording around border, bust portrait of Smith in center, 1 1/2" d...... **20**

Pinback button, stylized doves, celluloid, black & white, 1" d...... **15**

Pinback button, "We Shall Overcome," celluloid, black & white, 1 1/4" d...... **45**

Pinback button, "Young Peoples Jubilee - Bishop J.A. Hamlett," celluloid, black & white, photo bust portrait of the Bishop in center, wording around the border band, 1" d...... **75**

Poster, 3-D, "White Only/Black Only," 1968...... **75-100**

Poster, commemorative serigraph of Malcolm X, by Benjin, portrait of Malcolm X, 1967...... **200-350**

Poster, "Free Billy Smith," orange & black half-length sketch of black soldier in battle gear w/raised fist, reads in part "Let Our Brother Go! - Demonstration May 6," copy also reads "Billy Smith is on trial for fighting racism and oppression instead of the Vietnamese People," the demonstration planned at the Presidio in San Francisco, sponsored by the Northern California Coalition to Free Billy Smith, 1971, 11 x 17".. **70-80**

Poster, "Make Black Count," promoting black participation in the 1970 census, 1969-1970...... **75+**

Poster, Malcolm X, by artist Ernest W. Chambers, good likeness of the black leader...... **250+**

Poster, "Negro History Week - Twentieth Annual Celebration Beginning February 11, 1945," cardboard, large photograph of elderly Frederick Douglass, produced by the Association for the Study of Negro Life & History, Washington, D.C., 8 1/2 x 11" (light soil & stains, faint bend)...... **75**

Poster, "Racism Chains," artist Hugo Gallert, a black & white hand chained...... **125**

Poster, "Rev. Martin Luther King, Jr.," artist Erwin H. Cobb, 1967, date makes this piece rare...... **100-175**

Poster, "Revolutionary Intercommunal Day of Solidarity for Bobby Seale, Angela Davis and Post-Birthday Celebration for Huey P. Newton - Music by The Grateful Dead," Black Panther Rally, Oakland Auditorium, Oakland, California, 1971...... **150**

Poster, "Vote Baby Vote - Bay Area Urban League," black arm & fist clutching "ballot power" folded newspaper, 1968-1970...... **50+**

Poster, wanted-type, paper "WANTED by The FBI - Interstate Flight - Murder - Kidnapping - Angela Yvonne Davis," above two mug shots of the suspect, further description & details on lower half, 10 1/2 x 16"...... **250**

Potato masher, plastic handle & wire loop masher, yellow & blue, handle printed "NAACP - Freedom Fund," 1950s **105**

Program, "Announcing The Eastern Seaboard Conference of the Sojourners for Truth and Justice," cover art of Sojourner Truth by Charles White, call for meeting to work to free Mrs. Rosa Lee Ingram, produced by Charlotta Base, Vice Presidential candidate for the Progressive Party, March 1952, 4 pp. (foxing, edge wear) **42**

Program, "Democracy - The Challenge of Victory - An Invitation to the Sixth All-Southern Negro Youth Conference - Atlanta, GA - Nov. 30 - Dec. 1-2-3, 1944," large photo of young black couple on cover, instructions on application & housing, tentative program, history of organization & officers, four-page flyer, some foxing, minor soil, 8 1/2 x 11" **99**

Program, memorial, paper, "In Memoriam - Medgar Wiley Evers - July 2, 1925 - June 12, 1963," sponsored by the NAACP, photo bust portrait of Medgar Evers on front, his biography on back, 8 pages, 7 x 11" **80-90**

Record album, "March on Washington - The Official Album," long-playing, includes "Speeches by the Ten Civil Rights Leaders Heard at the Lincoln Memorial, Aug. 28, 1963," cover photo of the marchers, original copy of The March Pledge & an order form included, the group .... **100+**

Ribbon, commemorative, purple & gold, porthole-style bust portrait of John A. Andrews, Abolitionist Governor of Massachusetts during the Civil War, authorized creation of 54th Massachusetts 1st Colored Infantry, wording in lower portion "'I will never give up the rights of these men while I live, whether in this world or the next' - John A. Andrew," 7 1/2" l. **125**

Ribbon, convention, "GUEST - International - Brotherhood of Sleeping Car - Porters A.F.L. - First Triennial Convention - Los Angeles, California - Oct. 4-9, 1953," red w/printed lettering, 4" l. **50**

— Chapter 12 —
TOBACCIANA

A Large Collection of Figural Tobacco Humidors

Ashtray, bisque, figural outhouse w/black child on the commode inside, one side marked "Next" .... **$125+**

Ashtray, bronze-finished metal, nodding head-type, w/enameled standing figure of barefoot young black man colorfully dressed, 5" h **350-500**

Ashtray, ceramic, figural, large ashtray in the shape of a toilet .... **50+**

Ashtray, iron, picturing a black man's face in the bowl, inscribed wording "The man in the moon is a coon," rare, ca. 1915 .... **300-500**

Ashtray, porcelain, figural, plump black boy pulling small boy pushing wheeled toilet commode w/wooden cover .... **50+**

Ashtray, porcelain, figural, two black natives pulling & pushing cart in the form of a large die, red wheels & skirts & green grass base, Japan, ca. 1930s, 2 x 4 1/2", 3" h. (ILLUS. right) **28**

Ashtray with Black Natives

Ashtray stand, cast iron, floor model, full-figure black butler wearing frock coat, vest & bow tie, standing & holding wide shallow tray w/fins at each side to hold boxes of matches, very tall slender legs on square foot, decorated in red, black & white, ca. 1930s, 35" h. (overall paint crazing) **1,200**

Ashtray stand, cast iron, silhouetted figure of a black butler, red jacket, yellow vest, black pants, holds a long rectangular tray, early 20th c. (ILLUS. top right column) **750**

Black Butler Ashtray Stand

Ashtray stand, wooden, cut-out figure of black butler complete w/white spats holding glass ashtray, 35 1/2" h.. **350**

Figural Cigar Box Holder

Cigar box holder, ceramic, figural, designed to simulate rectangular cigar box w/well-dressed black man seated on top smoking cigar & wearing tan top hat, white shirt, blue cravat w/red dots & black pants & shoes, ca. 1970s (ILLUS.).................. **200**

Scarce "Booker T. Perfecto" Cigar Box

Cigar box, "The Booker T. Perfecto," color lithographed cardboard in light blue w/dark blue & red wording, inside of lid centered by round color portrait of Booker T. Washington above his facsimile signature, exterior edge wear, near mint interior, ca. 1920s, 8 3/4" l., 2 1/2" h. (ILLUS. bottom previous page) **537**

Cigar box label, lithographed paper, colorful scene of black man standing on oversized letter "L" for the brand "Lime Kiln Club," 5 1/4 x 7 3/8" (tiny tear in upper left) .... **175+**

Cigar holder, sterling silver, figural, modeled as black man wearing wide brimmed hat for holding matches, his body a large watermelon w/his feet sticking out the end, holding oval dished tray for ashes, back of watermelon open to hold cigars, ca. 1930s (ILLUS. below **$2,000**

Cigar humidor, cov., bisque, figural, bearded black man's head wearing fez w/blue tassel & bow tie .... **600+**

Black Porter Cigarette Dispenser

Cigarette dispenser, carved wood, figural, head of elderly black porter w/red hat, cigarette pops out of his mouth, ca. 1910-20 (ILLUS.) **350-450**

Cigarette dispenser, cast metal, figural, head of Josephine Baker, cigarettes pop out of her mouth .... **750+**

Silver Figural Cigar Holder-Ashtray

Cigar store stand-up, paper applied to plywood cut-out sign, bellboy w/bright red uniform, Charles Denby, ca. 1927 .... **600+**

Figural Cigarette Holder & Ashtray

Figural Black Men as Cigarette Holder & Humidors

Cigarette holder & ashtray, terra cotta, figural, black man seated on large basket holding barrel on one side & bowl-form basket on the other, naturalistic coloring, Austria, ca. 1920s (ILLUS.) **1,850**

Cigarette holder & ashtray, terra cotta, figural, black man seated on large basket holding barrel on one side & bowl-form basket on the other, naturalistic coloring, Austria, ca. 1920s (ILLUS. center with two figural black man humidors, above) **1,850**

Cigarette lighter, cast aluminum, figural, marked "Hot-cha," little black boy w/his pants down, the electric lighter placed in his posterior, marked "Made in U.S.A." (ILLUS. right) **300**

Cigarette lighter, metal, figural, Art Deco touch-tip, black bartender pictured with cocktail shaker, Ronson, sold originally for $22.50 in 1936, mint condition, 6" w. (ILLUS. top of next page) **1,500-2,000**

Cigarette lighter, metal, figural, Art Deco touch-tip, different version of black bartender pictured with cocktail shaker, Ronson, w/moveable compartment to hold ciga-

rettes in front, rarer version & commands more, 5 1/2" w. (ILLUS. with other bartender lighter top of next page) .... **2,500+**

Coupon, paper, for Nigger Hair Tobacco, expired June 30, 1914 .... **300**

Coupon, paper, for Nigger Hair Tobacco, expired June 30, 1915 .... **300**

Black Boy Cigarette Lighter

Rare Black Bartender Ronson Cigarette Lighters

Match holder, hanging-type, chalk, model of young black boy eating watermelon .... **250+**

Match safe, bisque, black male dancer, ca. 1890s, 4 1/2" h. .... **300+**

Wire Black Man Matchbox Holder

Matchbox holder, wire, figural, wire figure of black man riding wire bicycle w/front basket to hold small box of matches, zig-zag wire base, man w/wooden hat, red & white cloth shirt & tan cloth pants, slight soiling, 3 1/4 x 5 1/2", 6" h. (ILLUS.) **61**

Pipe, carved wood, alligator carved on the stem, black man behind the bowl w/stick in his hand & down alligator's throat, 12" l. .... **850+**

Pipe, clay bowl w/glossy glaze, molded in form of black man's head, shades of brown on cream, never used, about 2 x 3" (one side slightly soiled, small stem chips) **600**

Pipe rack w/match holder, carved wood, row of carved black men's heads on narrow shelf, inscribed "All coons look alike," ca. 1890s, rare... **2,000+**

Tobacco container, cardboard, "Bigger Hair" (changed from "Nigger Hair"). **300+**

Black Man & Watermelon Humidor

Tobacco humidor, all-bisque, figural, figure of black man seated holding large watermelon, Austria, ca. 1890s, rare (ILLUS. bottom right previous page) .... **2,000+**

Tobacco humidor, all-bisque, figural, model of black woman's head w/side curls & top knot tied w/green headbands, gold earrings, pale green collar w/purple bow, Germany, ca. 1920 (ILLUS. top right)......................... **450-800**

Tobacco humidor, all-bisque, figural, model of young black boy's head, his mouth open & crying, Germany, ca. 1920s (ILLUS. below left with other black children humidors).................. **450+**

Tobacco humidor, all-bisque, figural, model of young black boy's head w/smiling expression, Germany, ca. 1920s (ILLUS. below right with other black children humidors).............. **450+**

Tobacco humidor, all-bisque, figural, model of young black girl's head w/smiling expression, Germany, ca. 1920s (ILLUS. below center with other black children humidors)......... **400+**

Tobacco humidor, all-bisque, figural, model of young man's head in black & brown, Germany, ca. 1920s .... **450+**

Tobacco humidor, all-bisque, modeled as four different black baby faces peeking out of brown-spotted white stork's bundle, Germany, ca. 1920s (ILLUS. right)................... **450-650**

Figural Black Woman Humidor

Stork Bundle Tobacco Humidor

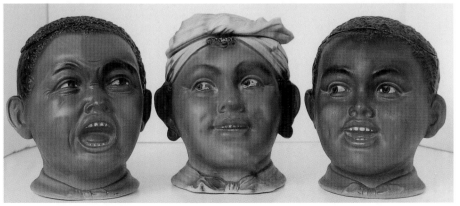

Humidors Modeled as the Heads of Black Children

Tobacco humidor, bisque, triangular upright form molded in relief on one side w/a black man playing cards, the legs molded as a grouping of tobacco pipes, the cover realistically molded as a deck of cards w/a die finial, hand-painted in color, Austria, ca. 1890-1910 (ILLUS. below) **1,800**

Tobacco humidor, ceramic, figural, large rounded head of a black man wearing a straw boater hat, can be inverted to show the same man grimacing & wearing a low cap, probably Germany, marked "JM 3470," ca. 1920s, 5 1/4" h. (ILLUS. bottom, photo of two views) **1,800**

Elderly Black Man Humidor

Tobacco humidor, ceramic, figural, modeled as head of bearded older black man, his soft fedora hat forming the cover, ca. 1890s (ILLUS.).... **1,200**

Tobacco humidor, ceramic, figural, modeled as head of light-complexioned brown-skinned woman w/turban top, Germany, ca. 1890s .... **450+**

Triangular Tobacco Humidor

Tobacco humidor, ceramic, figural, modeled as large round watermelon w/head of black man wearing top hat emerging through the top, marked "J.M. 8543," early 20th c. (ILLUS. at right with other figural black man cigarette holder & humidor page 227)... **1,800**

Two Views of Humidor Shaped Like a Man's Head

Smiling Black Boy Head Humidor

Tobacco humidor, ceramic, figural, modeled as realistic black boy's head, smiling & wearing pink double-brimmed hat & white shirt, Germany, ca. 1920s (ILLUS.) .... **800+**

Black Boy in Cotton Bale Humidor

Tobacco humidor, majolica, figural, the base formed as bale of cotton, the lid w/half-figure black boy wearing hat & holding pipe, ca. 1950s, 8 1/4" h. (ILLUS.) **800**

Tobacco humidor, painted terra cotta, figural, modeled as finely dressed black gentleman perched on large watermelon, Austria, marked "J.M. 8432," ca. 1890s, 9 3/4" h. (ILLUS. left with black man cigarette holder & humidor, page 226) **1,500**

Barrel & Black Child Humidor

Tobacco humidor, ceramic, figural, modeled as silver-banded brown barrel w/head of black child wearing red cap emerging at the top, ca. 1920s (ILLUS.) .... **800+**

Top Hat & Black Baby Humidor

Tobacco humidor, painted terra cotta, figural, modeled as large overturned top hat holding black baby, Germany, marked "J.M.," ca. 1890s (ILLUS. bottom right column previous page) ... **2,600**

Tobacco humidor, stoneware, advertising-type, "Old Green River Tobacco Co., Owensboro, Ky.," in the form of an old whiskey jug, marked "Old Green River - Smoke without a bite" **250**

Tobacco humidor, terra cotta, figural, black man wearing fez leaning on & looking over lectern at cat, marked "JM 2376," Germany, ca. 1900, 8 1/4" h. (ILLUS.) **2,500**

Rare Man Wearing Fez Humidor

Fine Black Man in Top Hat Humidor

Tobacco humidor, terra cotta, figural, bust of black man wearing top hat & holding small box in front, marked "JM 3326," Germany, late 19th - early 20th c., 10 1/2" h. (ILLUS.) **2,500**

Cotton Bale & Boy Tobacco Jar

Tobacco humidor, terra cotta, figural, cylindrical white bale of cotton w/rope top border, the lid w/half-length figure of black boy wearing blue shirt & red bandanna, marked "JM 3467," Germany, late 19th - early 20th c., 8 1/2" h. (ILLUS.) **518**

Boy Hugging Watermelon Humidor

Tobacco humidor, terra cotta, figural, modeled as seated black boy hugging large watermelon, signed "J. Nardi" (ILLUS. bottom right column previous page) .... **2,000+**

Black Man with Top Hat Humidor

Tobacco humidor, terra cotta, figural, robust black gentleman standing wearing a long coat & holding a top hat in one hand, marked "JM 8491," probably Germany, early 20th c., 8 1/4" h. (ILLUS.) **1,800**

Black Sailor on Barrel Tobacco Jar

Tobacco humidor, terra cotta, figural, young black sailor seated on upright half-barrel, red lips & white eyes, Germany, late 19th - early 20th c., 8 1/2" h. (ILLUS.) **690**

Watermelon-shaped Tobacco Humidor

Tobacco humidor, terra cotta, model of a large watermelon w/the facial features of a black man smoking a cigarette, probably Germany, marked "JM 3528," ca. 1920s (ILLUS.) **1,900**

Tobacco package, paper, chewing or smoking variety, labeled "Fiji Islander," 3 x 5" .... **100+**

Tobacco tin, cov., "Brilliant Mixture," rectangular, black & brown printed tobacco harvesting scene on cover, late 19th - early 20th c. (ILLUS. below) .... **350+**

"Brilliant Mixture" Tobacco Tin

— Chapter 13 —
TOYS & GAMES

Japanese Kobe Folk Art Toy

Animated folk art-type, rectangular base fitted w/half-length animated black man who cuts watermelon, tips his head & opens his mouth while lifting a watermelon slice, Kobe, Japan, early 20th c., excellent condition, 3 1/2" h. (ILLUS.) **$259**

Battery-operated, tin, "Strutting Sam," black man does jig on pedestal base, mint in box, 10 1/2" h. .... **550+**

Early Black Man Beanbag Game

Beanbag target game, lithographed die-cut cardboard, the head of black man w/mouth wide open to catch beanbags or wooden balls, ca. 1880s, splits at corners of mouth, very good condition, 13" h. (ILLUS.)... **230**

Bell toy, cast metal, alligator ridden by black native boy, late 19th c. .... **2,500+**

Card game, "Old Maid," cards w/six black characters, 1940s, the deck **45**

Clockwork mechanism, black boy orange seller, animated black youth sitting on cart & pushing it in an erratic movement, all-original w/no repairs or repaint, original paint & clothing w/slight soiling & one pant leg detached, w/original box w/illustrated label, Martin, early 20th c., 7" l. (ILLUS. bottom of page) **1,080**

Clockwork mechanism, Preacher, Ives Corp., late 19th c. **3,500-4,000**

Clockwork mechanism, tinplate, black dancer, Ives Corp., Bridgeport, Connecticut, ca. 1870s .... **3,000+**

Clockwork mechanism, tinplate, "New Century Cycle," three-wheeled vehicle w/white driver who lifts his hat (missing) while black boy in back seat turns the parasol, late 19th - early 20th c., Lehmann, Germany (ILLUS. top next page) **500-1,000**

Clockwork mechanism, Walking Black Man, Ives Corp., ca. 1870s, 9 1/2" h. .... **3,000+**

Early Clockwork Orange Seller Toy

Rare Clockwork Lehmann Toy

Friction-action, tinplate, "Africa," ostrich pulling cart w/black man holding reins, Lehmann, Germany, late 19th - early 20th c. .... **1,000+**

Game, board-type, "Little Black Sambo," first half 20th c. **300**

Game, target-type, "Ideal Patent," box cover w/flashily dressed black man pointing pistol at viewer, die-cut game pieces in color, one an American Indian chief on horseback, ca. 1930s, complete game, damage to box (ILLUS. of Indian Chief piece) **50**

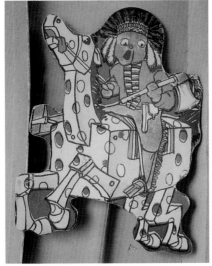

Piece from "Ideal Patent" Target Game

Figural Paper on Wood Game Pieces

Game pieces, figural, lithographed paper on wood, colorful depiction of standing black man w/mouth wide open holding large watermelon in front, fits on black wooden stand, early 20th c., each (ILLUS. of two previous page) **35**

Rare Early Jigsaw Puzzle

Jigsaw puzzle, "Chopped Up Niggers," colorful grotesque caricature box cover, by McLoughlin Bros., ca. 1910, complete in original box (ILLUS.) **1,500**

Jointed wood figure, model of African Chief wearing top hat & checkered pants, part of the Schoenhut Humpty Dumpty "African Safari" set, ca. 1910 .... **2,000+**

Jointed wood figure, model of African Drummer, part of the Schoenhut Humpty Dumpty "African Safari" set, ca. 1910 .... **2,100+**

Jointed wood figure, model of African Native, part of the Schoenhut Humpty Dumpty "African Safari" set, ca. 1910 .... **2,100+**

Jointed wood figure, model of the Negro Dude, wearing white top hat, dark coat & checkered pants, part of the Schoenhut Humpty Dumpty "Circus" set, ca. 1910, 8 3/4" h. .... **400+**

Jointed wood figure, model of the Negro Dude, wearing white top hat, dark coat & checkered pants, part of the Schoenhut Humpty Dumpty "Circus" set, ca. 1910, smaller sized version... **500+**

Marionette, plastic head & hands w/wooden feet & body, oversized head wearing primitive straw hat, shirt in white w/tiny blue flowers & orange & white check pants, 14 1/2" h. (slight soiling & wear).......... **88**

Movie film, "Little Black Sambo," 16mm, Castle Films, mint.................... **70**

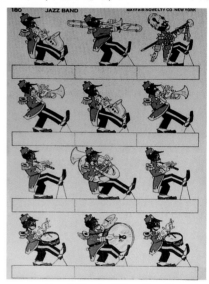

Uncut Sheet of "Jazz Band"

Paper cut-outs, "Jazz Band - Mayfair Novelty Co. New York," rows of black band members in colorful uniforms, ca. 1930s (ILLUS.)............. **35+**

Paper doll, advertising type, standing black Mammy wearing yellow & red plaid dress, white apron, white striped collar scarf & matching kerchief, early 20th c. **35**

Paper doll, advertising-type, black girl, for "Enameline - The Modern Stove Polish," base w/stand-up flaps, two-sided, girl wearing blue plaid dress & holding a white cat, another view w/an attached red dress & white apron pushing baby carriage, early 20th c............................ **45**

Black Cook & Dinner Paper Doll Set

Paper doll, black Mammy cook & her complete Thanksgiving dinner, full-page spread to cut out, from Delin- eator magazine, November 1912, the page (ILLUS.) **45**

Native Black Drummer Paper Doll

Paper doll, black native drummer, color paper cut-out, part of series illustrating story of Robinson Crusoe, from Ladies' Home Journal, 1918, the set (ILLUS. of drummer) **30**

Pull toy, metal, "Old Woman in a Shoe," Ives Corp., Bridgeport, Connecticut, late 19th c. .... **6,000+**

Black Man & Donkey Pull Toy

Pull-type, wood & pressboard, black figure w/top hat holding tail of kicking donkey, figure leans forward & donkey's ears move, Toy Tinkers, Evanston, Illinois, early 20th c., excellent condition, 10 1/2" l. (ILLUS.).... **201**

Puppet, painted & jointed wood w/paper-covered torso, jolly black minstrel man wearing red top hat & jacket w/black & white plaid bow tie, early 20th c. .... **150+**

"Ragtime Rastus" Record Doll

Record doll, jointed wood, "Ragtime Rastus," painted & jointed wood on platform, dances while record plays, early 20th c., w/original box (ILLUS.) **275-300**

Windup celluloid & cloth, "Poor Pete," young black boy holding slice of watermelon, a bulldog biting his posterior, Japan, ca. 1930s, paper label, working, 5 1/2" h. (ILLUS. left w/other "Poor Pete" toy top next page) **358**

Windup tin, "Alabama Coon Jigger," colorfully lithographed figure of a jointed black man above a rectangular platform base, w/original color-illustrated box w/original instructions & one spare rod, partial side flap missing, near mint, Lehmann, 1930s, 10" h. (ILLUS. next page) **1,080**

"Poor Pete" Windup Toys

"Alabama Coon Jigger" Toy & Box

Windup tin, "Alabama Coon Jigger," dancing black man, Ferdinand Strauss Corp., New York, New York, early 20th c., 9 3/4" h. .... **1,000+**

Windup tin, "Alabama Coon Jigger - Oh My," dancing black man, Lehmann, Germany, w/original box & instruction sheet, early 20th c. .. **1,000-1,200**

Windup tin, "Alabama Coon Jigger - Tombo," dancing black man, Ferdinand Strauss, New York, New York, ca. 1918, base 3 x 5", 10 1/2" h. .... **750+**

"Amos 'n' Andy Freshair Taxi Cab" Windup Toy

Windup tin, "Amos 'n' Andy Freshair Taxi Cab," orange w/black trim, Louis Marx, New York, 1930s, 8" l. (ILLUS. bottom previous page)........ **1,500**

Windup tin, Amos 'n' Andy walkers, moving eyes, Louis Marx, 1930s, 12" h., pr. .... **1,200+**

Windup tin, Amos 'n' Andy walkers, stationary eyes, Louis Marx, 1930s, 12" h., pr. .... **1,000+**

Windup tin, "Be-Bop - The Jivin Jigger," Louis Marx, New York, 1940s . **500+**

Black Clown Windup Tin Toy

Windup tin, black clown standing w/arms up & out, spins balls attached to ends of wires, marked "RF Japan," ca. 1920s (ILLUS.)................. **800**

Strauss Windup Black Porter Toy

Windup tin, black porter dressed in red pushes a green trunk that dog lurches out of, Strauss, 1930s, very good condition, 6" h. (ILLUS.)............. **600**

Windup tin, black porter pushing wheelbarrow, Ferdinand Strauss Corp., New York, New York, ca. 1920s, 6 1/4" h. .... **500+**

Windup tin, "Chicken Snatcher," black man holding chicken, dog biting seat of his pants, Louis Marx, 1920s.. **2,000+**

Windup tin, "Dapper Dan Coon Jigger," Louis Marx, New York, ca. 1920s.. **1,000+**

Windup tin, drummer boy, cloth-covered metal body w/stamped metal head, walks & beats drum, Germany, late 19th - early 20th c. .... **1,000+**

Rare "Ham and Sam" Windup Toy

Windup tin, "Ham and Sam - The Minstrel Team," upright piano w/seated player & standing man playing banjo beside him, Ferdinand Strauss, New York, New York, ca. 1920s (ILLUS.)............... **1,500**

Windup tin, "Hey-Hey The Chicken Snatcher," grotesque figure of black man w/chicken in one hand, a small dog nipping at his backside, face moves showing different expressions, Louis Marx, copyright 1926, all-original & working, 8 1/2" h. (ILLUS. top of next page)..................................... **1,200**

Marx "Hey-Hey Chicken Snatcher" Toy

Japanese Louis Armstrong Toy

Windup tin, "Jazzbo Jim," dancing man on roof of cabin, Ferdinand Strauss Corp., New York, New York, ca. 1920s........................... **600-700**

Windup tin, "Jazzbo Jim - The Dancer on the Roof," dancing man on roof of cabin, Louis Marx, ca. 1920s, 9" h.. **600+**

Windup tin, "Jazzbo Jim - The Dancer on the Roof," dancing man on roof of cabin, Unique Art, ca. 1930s........ **750+**

Windup tin, long alligator w/native on its back, J. Chein & Co., New York, New York, marked, ca. 1930s.......... **300+**

Windup tin, "Louis Armstrong Trumpet Player," the figure balances on one foot & kicks up leg, tips hat & blows a trumpet sound via an interior bellows, T.N., Japan, 1950s, excellent working condition, 10 1/2" h. (ILLUS. top of next column) .... **425+**

Windup tin, Mammy Shako Walker, Lindstrom Tool & Toy Co., Bridgeport, Connecticut, ca. 1930s............. **600+**

Windup tin, "Pango Pango," TPS, Japan, ca. 1950s, 6" h...................... **250+**

Windup tin, "Poor Pete," young black boy holding slice of watermelon, wearing red pants, white shirt & grey cap, a small dog biting his posterior, Germany, ca. 1930s, working, some scratches, 6 1/4" h. (ILLUS. right w/other "Poor Pete" toy, page 240).................................... **495**

Windup tin, "Sweeping Mammy," Lindstrom Tool & Toy Co., Bridgeport, Connecticut, ca. 1920s............. **500+**

Windup tin, "talking head," depicting dandified black man w/top hat, his articulated neck & jaw moving w/clockwork mechanism & cam driven to give him the appearance of guffawing, early 20th c., 7" h. **700**

— Chapter 14—

PHOTO GALLERY

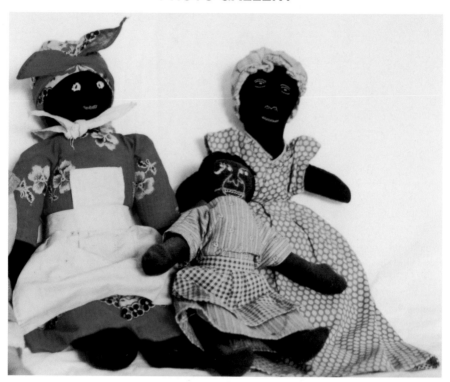

*Cloth dolls, late 19th or early 20th century, from left: mammy doll, 9" long, **$150-$180;** small black doll with detailed sewn face, 7" long, **$250-$300;** larger black doll, also a "topsy turvey" (when turned upside down she becomes a white doll), 11" long, **$150-$200.***

*Scootles, 13" black composition Scootles. Excellent condition in old clothes and replaced shoes. There is some peeling of paint on neck in back. **$400-$500***

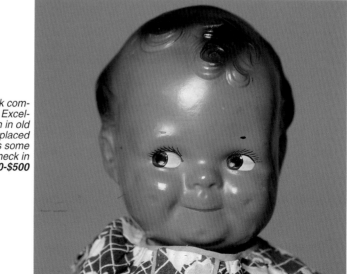

10" composition "ramp walker" black mammy that pushes a baby buggy, painted eyes and mouth, one arm has spring mechanism at elbow to allow it to hold onto buggy, wearing original polka-dot dress. **$75+**

22" black composition, cloth body with composition hands, plastic-covered flirty eyes, molded hair, wearing a white cotton dress. **$100+**

19" Black Paris Bé Bé (?)
Unmarked on rear of head
except for the number "8."
Head attached to body with
an inverted wood dowel.
The composition body is
fully jointed and has round
paper label on rear from a
Paris toy store. Amber set
paperweight eyes with red
lips and dark eyebrows.
Dressed in older velvet
costume and retains original nappy hair wig and cork
pate and antique leather
shoes. Body in extremely
fine original condition.
$5,000-$6.000

Black Poupée, 12" black
French F.G. Poupée. Dark
brown bisque and brown
leather kid body. Black wig,
wearing a costume made of
antique fabrics and striped
silk and red cotton with red
matching hat. Normal wear
to body. Minute scuff to tip
of nose and lower lip.
$1,300-$1,800

Black Character, 14" black S&H 1368 character. With open mouth, dressed in ethnic costume on a jointed French composition body. Wearing original nappy hair wig, with set light brown paperweight eyes. Antique clothing and shoes. Body overall is fine with minor wear to fingertips and at joints. ***$3,500-$4,000***

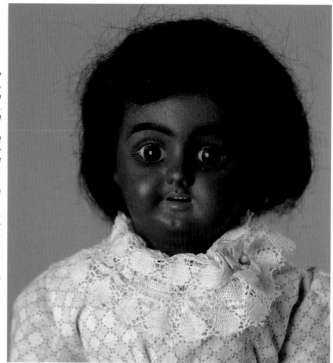

*German Child, 11 1/2"
German brown bisque
Simon and Halbig 739
child. Original choco-
late brown fully jointed
composition body.
Brown set eyes and
open mouth with four
teeth. Newly dressed
in blue and white cot-
ton with new shoes,
but still retains original
black mohair wig,
which has never been
removed. Wear at
neck socket where
there appears to be
some re-gluing to
shoulder seams.
$650-$750*

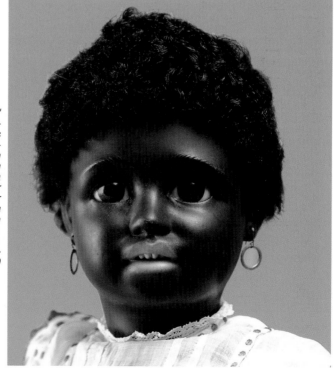

*Black Character, 22"
black S&H 1358 char-
acter. Brown set eyes
on a jointed composi-
tion body. Wearing an
antique white cotton
dress with red polka
dots, antique leather
shoes, and an older
curly black mohair wig
(wig has not been
removed from head).
Minor wear at joints.
Rare. $10,000-
$11,000*

Black Character Boy, 19" black smiling Van Rozen character boy. Dressed as a marquis and has marked French shoes (with bumblebee) and is wearing a white powder human hair wig and a three-cornered hat. Fully marked on rear of head "VAN ROZEN, FRANCE DEPOSE." Open lips exposing molded teeth. Inset dark brown eyes that are highlighted with painted black eyelashes. Overall body condition fine, minor chipping at elbows and one finger has been repaired. Rare. $12,000-$13,000

Sasha Black Baby,11" Sasha black baby. Black nappy hair with a white outfit, wrist tag, and original box. All original condition. $100-$125

Black Cora, 16" Trenton Sasha black Cora. All original, in original box with some yellow spots on dress. $100-$125

*Mammy jar with checked apron (paint touched up), 1950s, 11" tall, **$150-$200;** also comes in yellow and aqua. The bottom is marked McCoy and is glazed with a dry foot. Details on some examples are cold-painted on top of the glaze and show much wear.*

Left, genuine Mammy by Brayton Laguna, 12 3/4" tall, stamped "Copyright 1943 by Brayton Laguna Pottery," $600+. Right, reproduction Mammy, 11 7/8" tall, marked on the bottom with "30," and with a hand-written "W" inside base. There is a genuine Brayton Mammy with decoration similar to the zigzag pattern on the right, but the design is more uniform and the lines overlap.

Black Butler, Japanese, 7 1/2" tall, 1960s, ink-stamped "Made in Japan," handle missing. $1,000

*Mammy by Brayton Laguna, in rare red dress, 11 3/4" tall, 1940s, hand inscribed "Brayton 2" Adding to the confusion caused by reproductions is the fact that the genuine Brayton Laguna Mammy has been found in sizes up to almost 13" tall. With red dress, **$800-$900;** other colors, **$600+***

Herringbone Black Butler, Japanese, with rattan handle, 8 3/4" tall with handle down, early 1950s, ink-stamped "Japan." **$2,500+**

Mammy, Japanese, with rattan handle, 11 1/2" tall with handle up, 1960s, ink-stamped "Japan." **$1,000+**

Mammy, Japanese, 9 3/4" tall, 1950s, ink-stamped, "Made in Japan." Note black-glazed shoes, not common. **$600+**

Mammy biscuit jar, Japanese,
with rattan handle,
7 3/4" tall with handle down,
1950s, ink-stamped, "Japan."
$800+

Mammy biscuit jar, Japanese,
with rattan handle, 7 1/2" tall
with handle down, 1950s, ink-
stamped, "Hand Painted Japan
Maruhan Ware." **$900+**

Cauliflower Mammy, reproduction. **$25-$30**

Cauliflower Mammy, real jar with expected worn cold paint. (Prices for this jar once hovered around $1,000, but the reproductions have driven values down.) **$500-$600**

Mammy, in yellow, also found in white and aqua with cold paint decoration (widely available as a slightly smaller reproduction), 1950s, McCoy mark. (Rarely found with two other phrases around base: "Dem Cookies Sure Am Good" and "Dem Cookies Sure Got Dat Vitamin A.") **$200-$225**

Dem Cookies Mammy. There are many variations of the Mammy cookie jar. This one is the most sought after of all, because along the base it says, "Dem Cookies sho got dat Vitamin A." This version was not produced. This one, in a beautiful matte aqua, is supposedly one of only two in existence. **$4,000**

Washtub Mammy, attributed to Metlox, 11" tall, late 1940s, unmarked. **$1,800+**

Chef, by National Silver, with cold-paint highlights on mouth, 10" tall, 1940s, marked on bottom, "USA NSCO.) (Sometimes found with foil labels, and the mark "NASCO.") **$700+**

Mammy, by National Silver, with cold-paint highlights on mouth, 9 1/2" tall, 1940s, marked on bottom, "USA NSCO." (Sometimes found with foil labels, and the mark "NASCO.") **$700+**

Black Chef, by Pearl China,
marked in gold on front,
"Cooky," 10 1/4" tall, 1940s,
stamped on bottom, "Pearl
(in a seashell) China Co.
Hand decorated 22 kt. Gold
U.S.A." and impressed,
"639." (A companion to the
Chef was a mammy jar,
same marks, $900+.)
$600+

Aunt Jemima, plastic,
11 5/8" tall, 1950s, made
for Quaker Oats, marked
on bottom, "F&F." **$200+**

*Mammy, by Mosaic Tile Co. of Zanesville, Ohio (1894-1967), 13" tall, 1940s, unmarked, found in other colors. This example, **$750+;** other colors, **$500+***

This rare sepia-toned photo print titles "Alligator Bait," shows a row of charming black babies and toddlers. It was copyrighted in 1897. 6 1/2" x 20" **$259.**

Show at the top is the famous "Darktown Battery" Victorian cast-iron mechanical bank, **$1,840**; Below it is a folk art carved wood pipe with the bowl carved with the figure of a young black boy seated on a log with his rear end being nipped by an alligator, late 19th century, 9" l. **$690**.

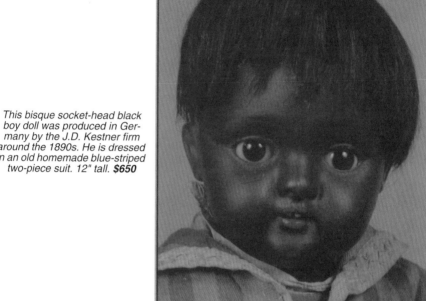

This bisque socket-head black boy doll was produced in Germany by the J.D. Kestner firm around the 1890s. He is dressed in an old homemade blue-striped two-piece suit. 12" tall. $650

J.D. Kestner of Germany produced this pretty brown bisque socket-head girl featuring brown sleep eyes and an open mouth with molded upper teeth. She wears a period eyelet dress & pinafore. 13 1/2" tall. $863

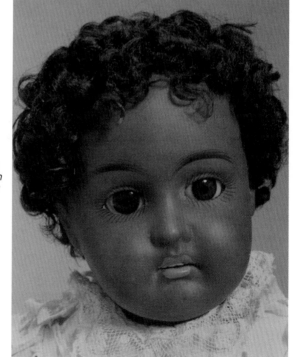

This lovely black lady doll was produced in the city of Limoges, France, in the late 19th century. She is elegantly redressed in a salmon and green French-style gown. Dating from around 1890, she stands 13" tall. **$550**

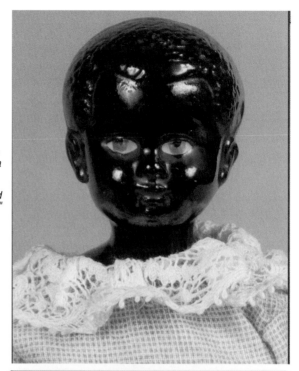

This black china head doll features painted brown eyes and a closed red mouth. The black cloth body has black bisque lower arms and legs. Unmarked and dating circa 1900, it is 9 1/2" tall. **$450**

The Armand Marseille company of Germany produced this Model 390 bisque head girl in the late 19th century. She features set brown glass eyes, an open mouth with four upper teeth and her original black mohair wig. She is nicely dressed and is 12 1/2" tall. **$385**

*This very rare late Victorian French-made automaton features a black gentleman with a bisque head and jointed body. When activated he raises his cigarette holder to his open mouth and inhales, then turns his head to the left slightly, looks upward and exhales the smoke. He also twists the wrist of his other hand and offers flowers to a lady. He is professionally redressed and stands on a tall box base enclosing a music box. 24" tall. **$5,750***

*These very elegant bronze and marble busts represent African natives named Nelusko and Silika. They were modeled by Luigi Pagani of Milan, Italy, and date from around 1871. The man is 38 1/2" tall and the lady is 34 1/2" tall. Value of the pair: **$321,000***

A wonderful large Victorian French automaton. This black gentleman has a bisque head and when activated he moves his arm with the cigarette holder to his mouth and inhales, then exhales the smoke. Redressed in an elegant outfit, he leans on a papier-mâché tree stump on a matching green platform. The deep black ebonized wood base conceals a music box. This piece was probably produced by Phailabois of France. 17" tall. **$4,300**

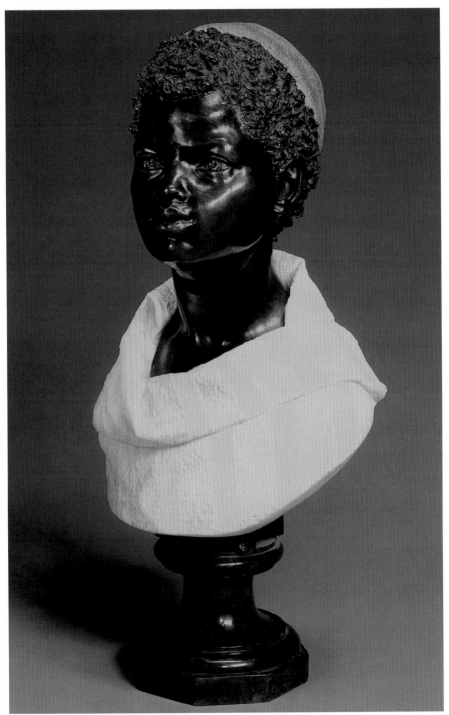

A beautiful bronze and marble bust of a young Nubian man wearing a red fez and striped robe. He was the work of a Raimondo Pereda of Milan, Italy, and dates circa 1880. His socle base is green marble. 16" tall. **$23,500**

*A remarkable life-sized terra cotta lamp produced in Austria by the F. Goldscheider firm. This North African servant boy wears a red fez, white shirt and brown pants and holds a candle. Dating from the late 19th or early 20th century, he stands 58 1/2" tall. **$16,730***

This lovely Art Nouveau style carved wood, gresso and polychrome figure of a female Blackamoor dancer was inspired by the famous dancer Loie Fuller. She wears an elaborate gown with a mask-head belt around her waist and stands on a tall matching carved white and gold pedestal. Likely produced in France, circa 1890, the overall height is 86" tall. **$4,830**

A unique very long-legged carved wood figure of an African-American redcap. He holds a tray and has an opening under his arm that possibly held a small bottle. There is also an opening in his back where a clockwork mechanism would have fit. He may also have been used as a smoking stand. made in the early 20th century he is 36" tall. **$500-$700**

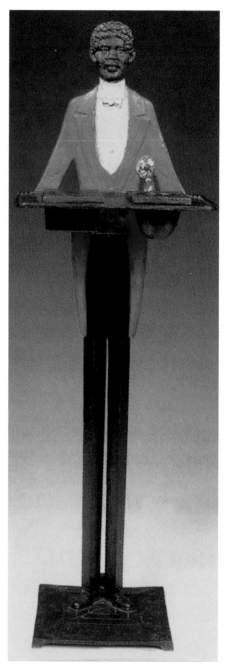

Shown here are two views of a fine carved rock crystal walking stick with a detailed bust portrait of a black man. The crystal shaft is joined to the makassar ebony shaft by a plain silver collar and horn ferrule. This 19th century piece was made in England and is 37 3/4" tall. **$2,070**

This figural cast-iron black butler smoking stand features the original paint. The figure holds out a rectangular tray with a covered cigarete box and ashtray. It dates from the 1920s and stands 33" tall. **$748**

This wonderfully detailed figure of an African-American laborer is actually made of fired pottery with realistic painted coloringl. He sits in a real wooden chair smoking a short cigar. This figure is reputedly one of 10 made from the New Orleans, Louisiana, exhibit at the 1900 World's Fair in Paris, France. Overall he is 51" tall. $7,188

This charming oil on canvas portrait shows a young African-American boy seated on a log smoking a cigar, his little dog seated beside him. It is unsigned but dates from the 19th century. The painting is 29" x 30" and in a modern frame with a gilt liner. **$2,530**

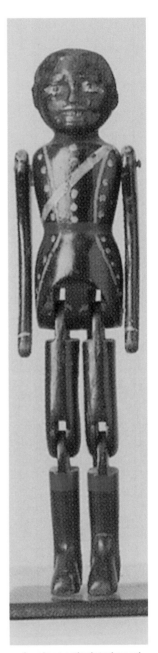

This rather unique cast-iron figural hitching post finial features a three-quarters length portrait of a young black man
with one hand on his hip. Finely detailed, it also features
traces of the original yellow paint. Dating from the second
half of the 19th century, it is 11 1/4" tall and rests on a later
octagonal wooden base. **$2,875**

A unique articulated wood
African-American dancing
man toy with its original
painted soldier's uniform. The
front half of the head is formed
of molded and painted gesso.
Probably made in the late 19th
century, it is 8 3/8" tall. **$403**

INDEX

Sample Size Aunt Jemima Flour Box

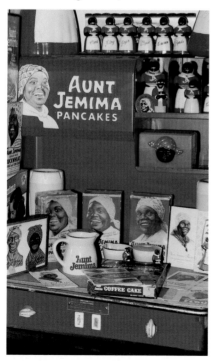

A variety of Aunt Jemima products atop a rare Aunt Jemima griddle

Tall Bisque Figure of Blackamoor Lady

Booker T

Brayton-Laguana, 11

Vertical French "Banania" Tray

Banania

Bergamont Hair Conditioner

Berry, Halle

Bill Robinson

Blackamoor

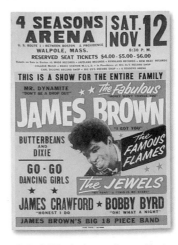

Colorful Early James Brown Poster

Brown, James

Bryant, Kobe

Famous Amos Cookie Bags

General Colin Powell - G.I. Joe Doll

Beam Decanter of John Henry

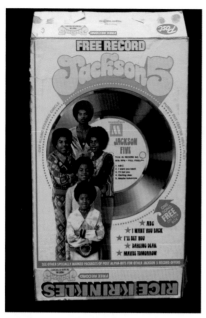

Jackson 5 on Frosted Rice Krispies Box

Scarce WPA Little Black Sambo Doll

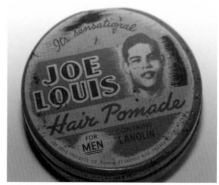

"Joe Louis Hair Pomade" Tin

Luzianne Coffee Salt & Pepper Shakers

Rare Polka Dot Mammy Candy Dish

Martin Luther King Jr. Commemorative Tin

Jackie McLean Record Album

McCoy Cylinder Cookie Jar

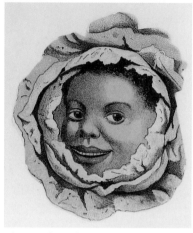

T

Tobacco Humidors

Large Uncle Tom & Eva Pottery Group

U

Uncle Tom and Eva

Urkel

Madam Walker's Hair Grower Tin

W

Walker, Madame C.J.

Williams, Vanessa

Woods, Tiger

Venus and Serena

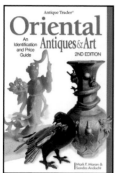

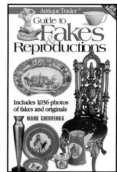
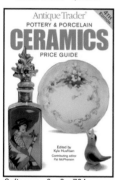
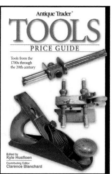
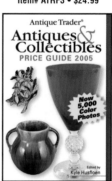

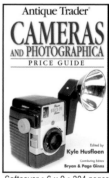